LETTERS OF AN ALTRURIAN TRAVELLER

LETTERS

OF

AN ALTRURIAN TRAVELLER

(1893-94)

BY

WILLIAM DEAN HOWELLS

A FACSIMILE REPRODUCTION

WITH AN INTRODUCTION

BY

CLARA M. KIRK

AND

RUDOLF KIRK

GAINESVILLE, FLORIDA
SCHOLARS' FACSIMILES & REPRINTS
1961

SCHOLARS' FACSIMILES & REPRINTS
118 N.W. 26TH STREET
GAINESVILLE, FLORIDA, U.S.A.
HARRY R. WARFEL, GENERAL EDITOR

REPRODUCED FROM A COPY IN
AND WITH THE PERMISSION OF

RUTGERS UNIVERSITY LIBRARY

L.C. CATALOG CARD NUMBER: 61-5081

WITH THIS BOOK
THE EDITORS PAY TRIBUTE TO
VASSAR COLLEGE
ON THE OCCASION OF ITS CENTENNIAL

MANUFACTURED IN THE U.S.A.
LETTERPRESS BY J. N. ANZEL, INC.
PHOTOLITHOGRAPHY BY EDWARDS BROTHERS
BINDING BY UNIVERSAL-DIXIE BINDERY

INTRODUCTION

William Dean Howells wrote for *The Cosmopolitan* twenty-three Altrurian essays between November, 1892, and September, 1894. The first twelve, forming a series entitled "A Traveller From Altruria," were re-issued as a book in 1894; the other eleven essays, called "Letters of an Altrurian Traveller," have never before been reprinted in full since their first appearance. Two of these Letters remained in *The Cosmopolitan* until the present; several are to be found, with deletions and alterations, in a volume of essays by Howells, *Impressions and Experiences* (1896); portions of others make up Part First of *Through the Eye of the Needle* (1907). The illustrations were not reproduced in these later printings.

Letters of an Altrurian Traveller is of interest to the reader today, because it offers him an opportunity to consider the candid comments of a sophisticated Traveller written to his friend in Altruria in the course of a visit to the United States in 1892-1893. In these Letters, Howells expresses his own criticism of America — sometimes caustic, sometimes humorous — at the time when he was at the peak of his long career.

After reading Tolstoy in 1885, Howells became deeply concerned with what he considered the selfish materialism of a burgeoning "plutocracy." His growing social awareness was reflected in a series of novels that began with *The Minister's Charge* (1887) and ended with *The World of Chance* (1893). *Annie Kilburn* (1888) was a direct reflection of the thinking stirred in Howells by reading *Que Faire?* by Tolstoy. Both Howells' novel, concerning an American girl's effort to bring social justice to a small New England town, and Tolstoy's long essay, presenting his observation of poverty when he was a tax collector in Moscow, became key contributions to the thinking of such men as Edward Everett Hale, Henry George, Richard T. Ely, Edward Bellamy, and W. D. P. Bliss. Howells, in turn, was influenced by the writing of all these men, for he was personally associating with them during his two years in Bostom, 1889-1891. While Benjamin Harrison was President, many reformers poured their energy into such movements as those of the Populists, the Nationalists, and the Christian Socialists. Howells' Altrurian essays were his response to these larger national currents, and were recognized in his day as relevant to the discussions roused by the rapidly changing economic scene in this country at the turn of the century.

Who, then, was the Altrurian?

I

THE ALTRURIAN IN *THE COSMOPOLITAN*

"Gentlemen, I wish to introduce my friend, Mr. Homos," said the popular novelist, Mr. Twelvemough, in the summer of 1892, addressing a banker, a minister, a lawyer, a doctor, and a professor, seated on the wide veranda of a country hotel in New Hampshire. Thus W. D. Howells presented a Traveller from Altruria to a group of Americans living in a decade torn with social strife; these gentlemen were at the moment thoughtfully enjoying their after-dinner cigars.

At the same time Howells introduced the readers of *The Cosmopolitan* to Aristides Homos, spokesman for his dream of an Altrurian America, and invited them to consider with him his hopes and fears for the expanding country. Mr. Twelvemough added, as further explanation of his guest: "Mr. Homos is from Altruria. He is visiting our country for the first time, and is greatly interested in the working of our institutions. He has been asking me some rather hard questions about certain phases of our civilization; and the fact is that I have launched him upon you because I don't feel quite able to cope with him."

By politely questioning the comfortable Americans whom he encountered vacationing in a summer hotel, and by conversing with the less fortunate Americans who lived on the impoverished farms near-by, Aristides Homos made it clear to the reader that he (and Howells) looked upon our competitive, business civilization as only partially evolved — in fact, as very near to a primitive state of barbarism. Many hundreds of years ago, the Altrurians, too, had passed through the Age of Accumulation, for they had lost sight of the Christian and Greek philosophy which they had known in their earlier, simpler days. They, too, had fought amongst themselves in pursuit of their selfish ends, but after generations of civic strife and useless warfare, they had come to understand that man destroys himself unless he accepts the basic concepts of Altruism. The beliefs of the early Christians, somewhat modified by the Greek love of beauty and respect for civil liberties, became once more the philosophy which guided the Altrurians in both their public and their private lives.

By means of this thinly-veiled satire on the plutocracy of the 1890's, Howells expressed his attitude toward strikes, money, war, religion, taxes, social snobbery, education, the family, the use of natural resources, and various other subjects then actually being discussed on many hotel porches. Though called on the title page "A Romance," *A Traveller from Altruria* (1894) ends with a long and serious speech by the visitor to the country people and summer boarders gathered at the New Hampshire resort.

Howells, as soon as he had concluded for *The Cosmopolitan* the series of Altrurian essays which make up the "Romance," began for the same publication a new series, entitled "Letters of an Altrurian Traveller." These Letters, eleven in number, appeared monthly between November, 1893, and September, 1894. Written by Aristides Homos to his friend Cyril in Altruria, the Letters reflect the Traveller's views of America, unmodified by his former urbane good manners.

INTRODUCTION

II

LETTERS I AND II

On September 1, 1893, the Altrurian, then in New York, writing a long letter to Cyril in Altruria, summed up the Traveller's impressions of America at the end of his first year in this country. This fantastic land seemed to him "like a belated Altruria, tardily repeating in the nineteenth century the errors which we committed in the tenth." This first Letter in the second Altrurian series was never included in any later publication by Howells, no doubt because the unvarnished views of "Babylon" — as the Altrurian now called New York — seemed to Howells, in retrospect, too outspoken.

Before the month was ended, an even longer letter went to Cyril, this time from Chicago, where Homos had journeyed to visit the great Columbian Exposition of 1893. This second Letter, likewise never reprinted, is of especial interest to the modern reader. In it is expressed the hope that the United States might eventually evolve toward the Altrurian vision of Classical beauty and Christian brotherhood which almost miraculously had become embodied in the White City on the shores of Lake Michigan. Aristides had always thought of Chicago as merely a sort of "ultimate Manhattan, the realized ideal of that largeness, loudness and fastness, which New York has persuaded the Americans is metropolitan." He added: "But after seeing the World's Fair City here, I feel as if I had caught a glimpse of the glorious capitals which will whiten the hills and shores of the east and the borderless plains of the west, when the New York and the Newer York of today shall seem to all the future Americans as impossible as they would seem to any Altrurian now."

Returning to New York two weeks later, he said, was like exposing himself "a second time to the shock of American conditions," unsupported by the "romantic expectations" which buoyed him up on his first arrival in this country. The weary Traveller confessed to his friend that he would like to take ship at once for his homeland and forget forever the harsh, competitive society of America. "But I have denied myself this," he wrote, "in the interest of the studies of plutocratic civilization which I wish to make." The comment on Chicago and New York which Aristides imparted to Cyril, enjoying the enlightened civilization of far-off Altruria, is clearly Howells' own view of the America of his day. Aristides is Howells' more critical self.

Howells himself paid a five-day visit to the Exposition in late September, 1893, as the personal guest of the Director, Daniel H. Burnham; he, as well as Aristides Homos, felt that the harmonious classical buildings of the Fair City, illumined by thousands of electric lights reflected in the lakes and lagoons of Jackson Park, suggested the neoclassical spirit of an earlier America. That this vision of ancient Greece should be brought within the range of the thousands of simple people from all parts of the country seemed to Homos-Howells a triumph of democracy. The New World thus declared to the Old that the outpost of civilization had moved to the West, for here in the heart of the industrial area Classical order and beauty had been brought into being by a mighty co-operative effort of selfless men and women working for the throngs who would come to view the wonders. They, in turn, would travel back to their small towns and villages, carrying the message of Altruism — or Christian brotherhood — modified by Classical balance and harmony. "The Fair City is a bit of Altruria"; to visit it is to wish to emulate it.

Howells was not alone in seeing in the Chicago Exposition this dream of the majestic future of the country. Hamlin Garland spent several weeks there, gathering material for his little volume of essays, *Crumbling Idols* (1894); Charles Eliot Norton made the tiresome trip from Boston and wrote home that the beauty of the Fair had renewed his hope for a national renaissance; though Henry Adams looked upon the Machine Age with foreboding, he returned to the Fair twice, so fascinated was he by the enchantment of the scene as well as by the dynamo in the Engineering Building. *Harper's Weekly, Century, Scribner's,* and all the other magazines and journals of the country dedicated whole issues to accounts of the Exposition. The entire December issue of *The Cosmopolitan* was turned over to articles on the White City and its implications for the future; Letter II of the second Altrurian series was Howells' contribution to this issue of the magazine. Through the Altrurian, Howells expressed his own concept of how innumerable Fair Cities might be built across the country, in spite of the selfish tendencies of our industrial civilization, for he had seen "the Altrurian Miracle" wrought in "the very heart of egoism," Chicago.

III

LETTERS III, IV, AND V

In order to consider the relationship of Letters III, IV, and V to their later re-appearance as two essays in *Impressions and Experiences* we must now go back several years in our story. Both "A Traveller From Altruria" and "Letters of an Altrurian Traveller" appeared as serials in *The Cosmopolitan* soon after that magazine was taken over by an aggressively social-minded editor from the West, John Brisben Walker. Because of Howells' prominence as a novelist and because of his social concern as expressed especially in *A Hazard of New Fortunes,* Walker had invited Howells in 1891 to become a co-editor of the new venture. By June, 1892, it was apparent to Howells that close association with "The Napoleon of the Magazines" (as the New York *Tribune* dubbed Walker) was, for him, impossible. However, the relationship between the two men, as editor and contributor, remained intact. Walker, who visited the Chicago Exposition on July 4, 1893, no doubt urged Howells to make a flying trip to the Fair and include his comments in the new Altrurian series beginning in the fall. Since Howells had written his last "Editor's Study" for *Harper's* just before he joined the staff of *The Cosmopolitan,* his Altrurian communications became Howells' monthly "voice," heard by an everwidening circle of *Cosmopolitan* readers. Under Walker the publication was challenging the pre-eminence of all the great New York magazines —

INTRODUCTION

even that of *Harper's*. It was Harper and Brothers, however, with whom Howells arranged for the issuing of "A Traveller From Altruria" as a book, for Walker's enterprise did not extend to a publishing house.

Why did not Harper also bring out in book form "Letters of an Altrurian Traveller?" Were the views expressed, especially in the first and second Letters, too strong for Harper and Brothers? We know only that the first two Letters of the group remained uncollected, though they contain some of Howells' most trenchant writing. We know, further, that Letters III, IV, and V did appear in 1896, as two essays in *Impressions and Experiences*, issued by Harper. The titles of the three Letters were then changed: "A Bit of Altruria in New York," "Aspects and Impressions of a Plutocratic City," and "Plutocratic Contrasts and Contradictions" became, when re-edited, "Glimpses of Central Park" and "New York Streets."

Not only were the titles toned down to suit the Harper public, but the Altrurian himself was removed from his Letters. These, of course, were no longer letters but essays admittedly written by Howells. We suddenly realize that the hotel into which the Altrurian retreated after his return from Chicago was near Howells' own West 59th Street apartment house, facing Central Park, where he lived at this time. That Howells himself had taken the place of the Traveller is evident at the very opening of Letter III, for there we discover one morning in October the author, and not the Altrurian, seated on a bench in Central Park, watching the sparrows and squirrels.

The Altrurian spent the winter at the old Plaza which, "preposterous" as he admits it is in structure, "forms a sort of gateway to the Park." The reader who troubles to compare, paragraph by paragraph, the original Letters with the re-edited essays will notice that columns of comment by the Altrurian on the filth of New York streets, the number of saloons on Sixth Avenue, and the poverty to be seen on any side-street, for example, have been deleted; he will notice, too, that many minor references to the beauty of Altrurian cities, the happiness of the people, and the part played by the government of Altruria, have also been omitted. It is important, then, to read Letters III, IV and V, as they first appeared in *The Cosmopolitan*, before they were edited for inclusion in *Impressions and Experiences*, because here the Altrurian's voice was more emphatic than Howells' own more restrained tone.

IV

LETTERS VI, VII, VII, X, X, XI

The remaining six Letters of the series lay forgotten in the bound volumes of *The Cosmopolitan* until they were resurrected by Howells to form Part First of *Through the Eye of the Needle* (1907), which was also a Harper publication. Though Howells, in preparing the volume, omitted some paragraphs, transposed others, modified sentences and phrases, he allowed the Altrurian to remain the speaker. The Letters, without superscriptures, now became essays, quieter in tone than the comments the Altrurian addressed to Cyril some fourteen years earlier, but unmistakably Howells' own.

INTRODUCTION

In an Introduction to the book written in 1907, Howells with ironic aloofness pointed out that it was the Altrurian, and not the editor, who was "entangled in his social sophistries." In offering this "synopsis" of the Letters written in 1893 to "an intimate friend in his own country," the editor indicated "certain peculiarities of the Altrurian attitude which the temperament of the writer has somewhat modified." Were the Traveller to visit us in 1907, Howells remarked with irony, his comment to his friend would surely have been altered. He would have noticed, for example, the present "munificence of the charitable rich"; "the general decay of snobbishness among us"; the quietness of Subway stations, now retreats "fit for meditation and prayer"; the sweet odors of traffic-filled thoroughfares; the disappearance of the old tenement houses, all of which are now modern apartments. Evictions have become so rare that, were the Altrurian to take a walk "in the poorer quarters of the town... in the coldest weather," he would probably not observe more than "half a dozen cases of families set out on the sidewalk with their household goods about them." The reader must bear in mind, said Howells, that when the Altrurian visited our country some years earlier, it was on the verge of a great depression which extended from 1894 to 1898. "But," remarked Howells, who was well known to his readers for his stand against the Spanish-American War of 1898, "Providence marked the divine approval of our victory in that contest by renewing in unexampled measure the prosperity of the Republic. With the downfall of the trusts, and the release of our industrial and commercial forces to unrestricted activity, the condition of every form of labor has been immeasurably improved, and it is now united with capital in bonds of the closest affection." As a result of those "bonds," we have long been enjoying a "sort of Golden Age, or Age on a Gold Basis."

With these sarcastic words Howells in *Through the Eye of the Needle* smoothly disentangled himself from responsibility for the views of the Altrurian. This 1907 Introduction is Howells' urbane but deeply satiric comment on the "prosperity" of the decade; it might well be considered one of his most important Altrurian essays.

Letters VI through XI were re-edited by Howells in 1907 to become Part First of his second Altrurian "Romance." A comparison of the original version with that in Part First of the *Needle* will show that Howells' editing meant the suppression of the more outspoken passages of the earlier essays, deletion of sentences and phrases in favor of milder comment, and, in the case of Letter IX, a drastic cutting and pasting in order to recombine it with Letter V. Apparently Howells had merely laid aside a section of Letter V which he later added to Letter XI.

The fact that Howells did not write Part Second until 1907 might explain the changes he felt he must make in Aristides' original Letters. Now the earlier Letters had to be brought into harmony with the new ending Howells found for his "Romance" when he reconsidered the sad fate which he had dealt Aristides in 1894. Eveleth Strange, who had decided at that time that she could not surrender her bank account in order to marry Mr. Homos, changed her mind in Part Second and with her mother pursued her lover to Liverpool, where they were married. The three then continued their outward voyage to Altruria. The brief chapters which Howells added in 1907 are the letters from Mrs. Homos to her friend Dorothea Makely in New York, reporting these romantic circumstances which must have happened many years before.

Eveleth Strange's decision to marry the Altrurian proves, one supposes, that a rich man — in this case a rich widow — can squeeze Through the Eye of the Needle. Eveleth's letters to her old friend, however, leave one in some doubt as to whether the whole experience — her marriage to Aristides, the serene sea voyage, the calm and happy existence on this mythical Island — was not, in fact, a dream. Howells, at the age of seventy, was willing to recast his earlier hope for the social redemption of the country in terms of vision, for he had come to feel less reliance on the power of "human nature" ever to change. As the old New York butler, who by chance found himself in Altruia, observed to Mrs. Homos, "It's rum here, because, though everything seems to go so right, it's against human nature." Eveleth promptly queried, "Then you don't believe a camel can ever go through the eye of a needle?" "I don't quite see how, ma'am," replied Robert, voicing Howells' own mistrust of the dream which, in the 1890's, seemed to him not entirely visionary.

V

A CYCLE OF AMERCAN THOUGHT

Letters of an Altrurian Traveller, as it came from the sharp pen of Aristides Homos in 1893-1894, is a link between Howells' two published Altrurian romances, and makes more clear the thought of their author in the last decade of the nineteenth century and the first decade of the twentieth. *A Traveller From Altruria, Letters of an Altrurian Traveller,* and *Through the Eye of the Needle* supply the necessary background for an understanding of the many novels, from *Annie Kilburn* to *The Son of Royal Langbrith,* which Howells wrote during the twenty-year span marking the height of his creative life. Only by studying the Altrurian essays in the form in which they were written can one understand Howells' protracted reflections on the social, religious, and political currents of his day.

One suspects that the romance of the Island of Altruria, which was called forth with something of Prospero's magic touch, enchanted the readers of Howells' generation, as it does our own. It is to be noticed, however, that Howells, like Shakespeare, was shrewdly aware of the world immediately around him; "A Traveller From Altruria" began to appear in the autumn of 1892, just when the country stood on the verge of an economic depression, which lasted until 1898, and *Through the Eye of the Needle* came out in April, 1907, a few months after the beginning of the Wall Street crash of that year which ushered in another great depression. The basic concepts of the two books remained the same, though vast changes had taken place in this country between 1892 and 1907. As Howells wrote in 1909 in a Preface to his "two romances," when he thought of putting them together in one book for the projected Library Edition of his works: "The two romances grouped here are books of one blood, but in birth so far divided from each other by time that they might seem mother and daughter rather than sisters. Yet they are of the same generation and born of the same abiding conviction: the conviction that the economic solution of the 'riddle of the painful earth' is to be by emulation and not by competition." Together these romances express Howells' "vision of idealities," which "must one day be the actualities of the world."

Letters of an Altrurian Traveller holds an important place in the long line of Altrurian essays which reflect Howells' brooding thought on the "riddle of the painful earth." Christian in concept, Classical in tone, it is sharply critical of the actual economic and social conditions of our country during the Age of Accumulation before the First World War.

That Howells' meditations on travellers from afar who bring enlightenment never ceased is attested by the last "Easy Chair" he wrote for *Harper's*, April, 1920, before his death the following month. Here two visitors from Mars bring news of their planet, which is "entirely socialized," where war is unknown and civic harmony prevails. When the Editor suggests that his visitors describe their life on this fortunate planet to a gathering of his fellow citizens in a large public hall, he adds the warning: "Be careful, though, about your socialization. Socialism isn't at all in favor just now. It was some time ago, when it was in the doctrinaire state — *Looking Backward* and the like — but now that we see the latter-day socialists really mean it — well, it's another thing. See? Better confine yourselves to your material conditions — your canals and inland seas and polar snow-caps. Don't touch on moral or economical affairs."

The New York audience, which crowded a large lecture hall to hear the Martians speak, soon decided that it would be unsafe indiscriminately to admit visitors from neighboring planets and that the two guests should be deported. Means for returning them to Mars, however, were not then available; "as the next best thing," Howells tells us in conclusion, "they were sent to Russia upon the theory that they were Bolshevists."

Thus Howells in his "vision of idealities" commented on a cycle of American thought from Christian Socialism to the Russian Revolution. His tone, in the course of these thirty years, varied from that of the urbane observer to that of the caustic critic or the disillusioned ironist; it was always serious, for, in his effort to envisage an Altrurian America, he was concerned with his own social conscience, which, in a sense, was also the national conscience.

Clara M. Kirk
Rudolf Kirk

Rutgers University
May 10, 1960

By W. D. Howells.

I.

New York, September 1st, 1893.
My dear Cyril:

I hoped before this to have seen you again in Altruria, and given you by word of mouth some account of my experiences and observations in this country; but I have now been here more than a year, and I find myself still lingering here in a kind of fascination. At times I seem to myself to have been in a fantastic dream since I landed on its shores, with the spectacle of so many things before me happening without law and without reason, as things do in sleep; and then, again, it is as if I were carried by some enchantment back to the old competitive period in our own country; for, after all, America is like a belated Altruria, tardily repeating in the nineteenth century the errors which we committed in the tenth. In fact, if you could imagine an Altruria where the millennium had never yet come, you would have some conception of America; and, perhaps, I had better leave you with this suggestion, and not attempt farther to generalize from my impressions, but give you these at first hand and let you form your own idea of the American civilization from them.

I say civilization, because one has to use some such term to describe a state which has advanced beyond the conditions of cannibalism, tribalism, slavery, serfdom and feudalism; but, of course, no Altrurian would think America a civilized country, though many of the Americans are as truly civilized as ourselves. We should not think it a democratic country, though many of the Americans are really democrats, and they are all proud of their republican form of government, though it is now little but a form. Far less should we think it a Christian country, though it abounds in good people, who love one another, and lead lives of continual self-sacrifice. The paradox is intelligible when you reflect that these Americans are civilized, and democratic and Christian, in spite of their conditions and not because of them. In order to do them full justice, you must remember that they are still, socially as well as civically, sunk in the lowest depths of competition, and that, theoretically at least, they prize this principle as the spring of all the personal and public virtues. To us this is a frightful anomaly; but because they do not feel it so, they are often able to do and to will the good, as I have intimated. Nowhere else in the whole world is capitalism now carried to such brutal excess, and yet nowhere else have qualities which we should think impossible in a capitalistic state shown themselves so nobly, so beautifully. It is this fact, in its different aspects, which, I suppose, has formed for me that fascination I have felt almost from the first moment of my arrival.

I had hardly been in the country a week before an illustration of the facility with which human nature adjusts itself to bad conditions and makes them tolerable by its patience, eclipsed all the little instances that were every moment offering themselves to my notice. The great event at Homestead, which our Altrurian papers will have given you some account of, occurred little over a year ago, but it is already forgotten. To the Americans it was not astounding that a force of armed workmen should bloodily fight out their quarrel with the mercenaries of their masters. In many states no change of the laws in respect to the incident has taken place to prevent its repetition, on any larger or smaller scale. None of the legal procedures have resulted in anything, and so far as the arrests for murder on either side are concerned, the whole affair has ended like a comic opera; and the warring interests have left the stage singing the same chorus together. The affair is, in fact, so thoroughly bouffe that I have to take my imagination in both hands before I can conceive of it as a fact; but the Americans are so used to these private wars between the banded forces of labor and the hirelings of capital, that they accept it as something almost natural, or as a disease inherent in the nature of things, and having its own laws and limitations. The outbreak at Homestead, as you know, was followed by something like a civic convulsion among the miners in Tennessee and in Idaho, and by a strike of railroad employés at Buffalo, which destroyed immense values, delayed traffic, and shed blood on both sides. In this last strike it was thought a great gain that the railroad managers, instead of employing mercenaries to shoot down the strikers, appealed to the state for protection; and it was somehow felt to be a fine effect of patriotism that the militia should occupy the scene of the riot in force and bear themselves toward the strikers like the invaders of an enemy's country.

If it had not all been so tragical in other aspects, the observer must have been amused by the attitude of most Americans towards these affairs. They seemed really to regard them as proofs of the superiority of the plutocracy which they call a republic, and to feel a kind of pride in the promptness and ferocity of the civil and military officials in suppressing symptoms which ought to have appealed to every sane person as signs of the gravest organic disorder. To my mind nothing seems so conclusive against their pretensions to civilization as the fact that these terrible occurrences are accepted as the necessary incidents of civilization.

There was, indeed, a certain small percentage of the people who felt the significance of the disasters; and I am anxious to have you understand that the average of intelligence among the Americans, as well as the average of virtue, is very high, not according to the Altrurian standard, of course, but certainly according to the European standard. Bad as their plutocracy is, it is still the best system known to competitional conditions, except perhaps that of Switzerland, where the initiative and the referendum enable the people to originate and to ultimate legislation, while the Americans can do neither. Here, the people, as you know, can only elect representatives; these again delegate their powers to committees, which in effect make the laws governing the nation. The American plutocracy is the old oligarchic conception of government in a new phase, and while it is established and maintained by a community mostly Christian, it is essentially pagan in its civic ideal. Yet this people, whose civic ideal is pagan, are, many of them, not only Christian in creed, but Christian in life, so far as their polity and their society permit them to think rightly and act generously. There are beautiful and pathetic instances of approach to our ideal among them which constantly win my admiration and compassion. That is to say, certain Americans are good and gentle not because of conditions that invite them to be so, but in spite of conditions that invite them to be otherwise, almost with the first economic and social lessons which they teach. Almost from the beginning the American is taught to look out for himself in business and in society, and if he looks out for others at the same time it is by a sacrifice of advantages which are vitally necessary to him in the battle of life. He may or he may not make these sacrifices; he very often does, to such effect that the loveliest and lovablest natures I have known here have been those of unsuccessful Americans, and the ugliest and hatefullest, those of successful Americans. But the sad thing, and the droll thing, is that they think their bad conditions the source of their virtues, and they really believe that without the inducements to rapacity on every hand there would be no beauty in yielding and giving.

Certain persons have been instanced to me as embodying certain generous qualities, and when I explain that the man who had not all these qualities in Altruria would be as exceptional as the man who has them is here, I have seen that people either did not believe me or did not understand me. The Americans honor such qualities as much as we do, and they appreciate gentleness, unselfishness, and neighborliness as much as we do, but they expect them only so far as they do not cross a man's self-interest; when they do that, he is a very unusual man if he continues to indulge in them, or, as they say, he is not *business*. When I tell them that the man who does not indulge them in Altruria is not business they look blank, or suspect me of a joke. When I try to make them understand that in their sense we have no self-interest in Altruria, and that if they had our conditions they would have no self-interest, it alarms them; they have so long been accustomed to live *upon* one another that they cannot imagine living *for* one another; they think self-interest a very good thing, the best sort of thing, and they ask what merit has a man in being good if he is not good to his disadvantage; they cannot conceive that a man *should* have no merit in being good. As for Christ's coming to do away with the old pagan economics as well as the old pagan ethics, they hoot at the notion.

I will not try, in this letter, to tell you just how all this can be; you will, in some sort conceive of its possibility from what you know of the competitive world at second hand, but I hope to make it clearer to you by and by. You must always account for a sort of bewilderment in me, inevitable in the presence of a state of things which is the complete inversion of our own, and in which I seem to get the same effect of life that boys sometimes get of the landscape by putting down their heads and looking at it between their legs.

Just at present there is no violent outbreak in the economic world, no bloody collision between labor and capital, no private war to be fought out in the face of the whole acquiescent nation till the inconvenience forces the government to interfere and put down the weaker party. But though there is now an interval of quiet, no one can say how long it will last, and many feel that there is even something ominous in it, that it is something like the calm in the heart of the cyclone. The cyclone is financial, if I may carry out the figure, and it began to blow, no one knows why or whence, several months ago. A great many weather-wiseacres pretended to know, and began to prophesy that if the export of gold to Europe could be stopped, and the coinage of silver could be arrested, and the enormous imposts could be removed, the ship of state would have plain sailing again. But the outflow of gold ceased without the slightest effect upon the cyclone; the mere threat of touching the tariff caused the closure of factories and foundries by the score, and the otiosation of workmen by the hundred thousand; with every prospect that the coinage of silver would be arrested, there were failures of banking-houses and business-houses on every hand. It remains to be seen what effect the actual demonetization of silver will have upon the situation, but the situation is so chaotic that no one among all the weather-wiseacres ventures to prophesy when the storm will cease to rage. Perhaps it has already ceased, but so far as the logic of events is concerned we might as well be in the heart of the cyclone, as I suggested.

I am afraid that with all your reading, and with all your special study of American conditions you would be dismayed if you could be confronted with the financial ruin which I find myself in the midst of, but which this extremely amiable and hopeful people do not seem to think so desperate. Like their bloody industrial wars, it is of such frequent recurrence that they have come to look upon it as in the order of nature. Probably they would tell you, if criticised from our point of view, that it was human nature to go to pieces about once in so often, and that this sort of disintegration was altogether preferable to any hard and fast system that held it together by the cohesion of moral principles. In fact their whole business world is a world of chance, where nothing happens according to law, but follows a loose order of accident, which any other order of accident may change. The question of money is the prime question of American life, and you would think that the issue of money would be one of the most carefully guarded functions of the government. But curiously enough, most of the money in the hands of the American people is not issued by the government at all, but consists of the promissory notes of a multitude of banks, as was the case with us in the old competitive days. The government bonds, which perpetuate the national debt, that their circulation may be based on them, are exempted from taxation as a sort of reward for the usurpation of the governmental function by the banks; and these banks are supposed to serve the community by supplying business men with the means of carrying on the commercial warfare. But they do this only at the heaviest rates of interest, and in times of general prosperity: at the first signs of adversity they withhold their favors. You might think that the government which secures their notes would also secure their deposits, but the government does nothing of the kind, and the man who trusts his money to their keeping does so wholly at his own risk. When they choose, or when they are unable, they may cease to pay it back to him, and he has no recourse whatever.

With a financial system resting upon such a basis as this, and with the perpetual gambling in values, nominal and real, and in every kind of produce and manufacture, which goes on throughout the whole country, you can hardly be surprised at the recurrence of the panics which follow each other at irregular intervals in the American business world. Indeed, the Americans are not surprised themselves; they regard them as something that always must be because they always have been, though they own that each successive panic spreads wider disaster and causes deeper suffering. Still, they expect them to come, and they do not dream of contriving a system like ours, in which they are no more possible than human sacrifices. They say, that is all very well for us Altrurians, but it would not do for Americans, and they really seem to believe that misery on so vast a scale as they have it in one of their financial convulsions is a sort of testimony to their national greatness. When they begin to drag themselves up out of the pit of ruin, bewildered and bemired by their fall, they begin to boast of the magnificent recuperative energies of the country. Still, I think that the old American maxim that it will all come out right in the end, has less and less acceptance. Some of them are beginning to fear that it will come out wrong in the end, if they go their old gait, or that it will at least come out Europe in the end. I would not venture to say how common this doubt was, but it certainly exists, and there is no question but that some of the thoughtfulest and best Americans are beginning to look toward Altruria as the only alternative from Europe.

Such Americans see that Europe is already upon them in the conditions of the very rich and the very poor. Poverty is here upon the European terms, and luxury is here upon the European terms. There is no longer the American workingman as he once was; he still gets better wages than the European workingman, but his economic and social status is exactly the same. He has accepted the situation for the present, but what he intends to do about it hereafter, no man knows; he, least of all men, knows. The American plutocrat has accepted the situation even more frankly than the proletarian. He perceives distinctly that there is no American life for the very rich American, and when he does not go abroad to live, as he increasingly does, he lives at home upon the same terms and to the same effect that the Continental noble lives in Europe; for the English noble is usefuller to his country than the rich American. Of course the vast majority of Americans are of the middle class, and with them you can still find the old American life, the old American ideals, the old American principles; and if the old America is ever to prevail, it must be in their love and honor of it. I do not mean to say the American middle class are as a general thing consciously American, but it is valuable that they are even unconsciously so. As a general thing they are simply and frankly bent upon providing for themselves and for their own; but some of them already see that they cannot realize even this low ideal, as things are, and that it will be more and more difficult to do so hereafter. A panic like the present is a great object lesson to them, and teaches the essential insecurity of their system as nothing else could. It shows that no industry, no frugality, no sagacity can be proof against such a storm, and that when it comes, the prudent and the diligent must suffer from it like the imprudent and the indolent. At last some of them are asking themselves if there is not something wrong in the system itself, and if a system based upon self-seeking does not embody recurrent disaster and final defeat. They have heard of the Altrurian system, and they are inquiring whether the sole economic safety is not in some such system. You must not suppose their motive is so low as this makes it seem. They are people of fine courage, and they have accesses of a noble generosity, but they have been born and bred in the presence of the fact that each man can alone save himself and those dear to him, from want; and we must not blame them if they cannot first think of the beauty and the grandeur of saving others from want. For the present, we cannot expect that they will think of anything higher at first than the danger to themselves, respectively; when they grasp the notion of escape from that, they will think of the danger to others, and will be eager to Altrurianize, as they call it, for the sake of the common good as well as the personal good. I may be in error, through my zeal for Altrurian principles, but I think that the Altrurian idea has come to stay, as they say, with this class. At any rate, it is not the very rich or the very poor who are leading reform in our direction, but it is such of the comfortable middle class as have got the light. There is everything to hope from this fact, for it means that if the change comes at all, it will not come superficially and it will not come violently. The comfortable Americans are the most comfortable people in the world, and when they find themselves threatened in their comfort, they will deal with the danger seriously, deliberately, thoroughly.

But whatever the struggle is to be here, whether it will be a wild revolt of the poor against the rich, of laborer against capitalist, with all the sanguinary circumstance of such an outbreak, or whether it will be the quiet opposition of the old American instincts to the recent plutocratic order of things, ending in the overthrow of the pagan ideals and institutions, and the foundation of a commonwealth upon some such basis as ours, I am sure that some sort of conflict is coming. I may be unable to do the proletarians justice, but so far, I do not think they have shown great wisdom in their attitude. If you were here you would sympathize with them, as I do in their strikes; but I think that you too would feel that these were not the means to achieve the ends they seek, and that higher wages and fewer hours were not the solution. The solution is the complete control of the industries by the people, as we know, and the assurance to every man willing to work that he shall not want; yet I must confess that the workingmen in America have not often risen to the conception of this notion. It is from those who have not been forced to toil so exhaustively that they cannot think clearly; it is from the comfortable middle class, which sees itself more and more closely environed by the inimical factors of this so-called civilization that the good time is to come. It is by no means impossible, indeed, if things should now go on as they are going, and the proletarians should be more and more subjected to the plutocrats, that we should find the workingmen arrayed by their enemies against the only principles that can befriend them. This is to be seen already in the case of those small merchants and manufacturers whose business has been destroyed by the trusts and syndicates, but who have been received into the service of their destroyers; the plutocracy has no such faithful allies and followers. But it is not possible for all the small merchants and manufacturers to be disposed of in this way, and it is to such of these as perceive the fact, that the good cause can look for help. They have already fully imagined the situation, and some of them have imagined it actual. It is chiefly they, therefore, who are anxious to Altrurianize America, as the sole means of escape from their encompassing dangers. Their activity is very great and it is incessant ; and they were able to shape and characterize the formless desires of a popular movement in the West, so that at the last presidential election twenty-two electoral votes were cast in favor of the Altrurian principles which formed the vital element of the uprising

Nevertheless, as I have more than once suggested, I do not think any fundamental change is near. The Americans are a very conservative race, and much slower to move than the English, as the more intelligent English have often observed. The Altrurianization of England may take place first, but I do not think I am mistaken in believing that America will yet be entirely Altrurianized. Just at present the whole community is proletarianized, and is made to feel the poor man's concern as to where the next day's bread or the next day's cake is to come from ; if a man is used to cake he will be as anxious to keep on having cake as the man who is used to having bread alone will be anxious to keep on having bread. In former times this experience would probably have been without definite significance or ultimate effect, but now I do not think it will be so. The friends of Altrurianization will be sure to press its lessons home ; and the people have been so widely awakened to the possibility of escape from the evils of their system that they will not be so patient of them as they have been in former times.

You might infer from the apparently

unbroken front that the Americans show on the side of competition in the great conflict dividing every nation into opposing camps, that there was no division amongst them. But there is very great division amongst them, and there is acceptance of one Altrurian principle or another to such a degree that there may be said to be almost a universal tendency toward Altrurianization, though, as a whole, the vast majority of Americans still regard the idea of human brotherhood with distrust and dislike. No doubt they will now patch up some sort of financial modus vivendi, and go on as before; in fact, there is no reason why they should not, in their conception of things. There was no reason why the panic should have come, and there is no reason why it should not go; but still, I do not think it will have come and gone without something more of question than former panics.

The friends of Altrurianization will not fail to bring before the American people some question of the very nature of money, and of the essential evil of it, as they understand money. They will try to show that accumulated money, as a means of providing against want, is always more or less a failure in private hands; that it does not do its office; that it evades the hardest clutch when its need is greatest. They will teach every man, from his own experience and conscience, that it is necessarily corrupting; that it is the source of most vices, and the incentive, direct or indirect, of almost every crime. They will prove that these are not the mere accidents of money, but are its essentials; and that a thing invented to create or to recognize economic inequality among men can never be otherwise than hurtful to them. They will preach the Altrurian notion of money, as the measure of work done and the warrant of need to be relieved, which in a civilized state can have no use but to issue from the commonwealth to the man who has worked, and return to the commonwealth from the man who has satisfied his wants with it. As yet, most Americans believe that money can be innocently gathered into one man's hands by his cunning and his skill, and as innocently taken from another's through his misfortune or his weakness. This primitive notion of money, which is known to us historically, is of actual effect among them; and though I was aware of the fact before I came to America, as you are now, I had no idea of the infernal variety of the evil.

In Altruria we cannot imagine a starving man in rags, passing the threshold of another man surfeited with every luxury and warranted in his opulence by the same law that dooms the beggar to destitution. But this is a spectacle so common in this great typical American city that no one would turn to look at it. In fact, both the beggar and the millionaire recognize the situation as something almost normal. Charity, the love of man and the fear of God, as the Americans know it, does not propose to equalize the monstrous conditions, or to do more than afford alleviation at the best, until the wretch in the gutter can somehow win from the wretch in the palace the chance to earn a miserable wage. This chance is regarded not as his right; it is his privilege, and it is accorded him usually at the cost of half a dozen other wretches, who are left outcast by it. It is money that creates this evil, and yet the Americans think that money is somehow a good thing; and they think they are the most prosperous people on earth, because they have more moneyed men among them than any other people.

I know, my dear Cyril, how strange all this will seem to you, how impossible, in spite of your study of American conditions. I remember how we used to talk of America together, before I planned my present visit, and how we disputed the general Altrurian notion of this country, as necessarily mistaken, because we said that such things could not be in a republic and a democracy. We had our dreams of a system different from ours, a system which vaunted itself the realization, above all others, of the individuality which we Altrurians prize more than everything else. We felt that our emissaries must have been hasty or mistaken in their observations, but you have only to visit this democratic republic, to understand that they have no such thing as individuality here, and that in conditions where one man depends upon another man for the chance of earning his bread, there can be no more liberty than there is equality.

The Americans still imagine that they have liberty, but as for the equality which we supposed the aim of their democracy, nobody any longer even pretends that it is, or that it can be. With the rich there is a cynical contempt of it; with the poor a cynical despair of it. The division into classes here is made as sharply as in any country of Europe, and the lines are passed only by the gain or the loss of money. I say only, but of course there are exceptions. The career is still open to the talents, and the plebeian rich here are glad to ally themselves with the patrician poor of Europe; but what I say holds good of the vast majority of cases. Every tendency of economic and social life is a tendency to greater and greater difference between the classes; and in New York, which is the most typical of American cities, the tendency is swifter and stronger than in other places.

It is for this reason that I have come here for the winter before I leave these shores, as I hope, forever. My American sojourn has been a passionate disappointment from first to last: it has been a grief which I cannot express to you, for the people are at heart so noble, so generous, so magnanimous, so infinitely better than their conditions that my pity for them has been as great as my detestation of the terms on which they accept life. I cannot convey to you the pathos with which the spectacle of their contradictions fills me; I can only say that if I were an American with nothing but a competitive conception of life, as a warfare in which the strong must perpetually and even involuntarily oppress the weak, as a race in which the swift must seize every advantage of the slow, as a game in which the shrewd must outwit the simple, I would not accept life at all. But, of course, I speak as an Altrurian, and I warn you that an utter abhorrence of the situation would ignore a thousand things that are lovely and of good report. It would ignore the most heroic self-sacrifice, the most romantic martyrdom, the spectacle of unnumbered brave and good, who do not the less sublimely lay their hearts upon the altar, because they lay them futilely there.

It is the exceptional character of what is generous and noble in the Americans, this accidental, this vicarious nature of their heroism and their martyrdom, that moves me to a pity for which there seems no relief but laughter. They pray as we do that God's will may be done here, and His kingdom come on earth as it is in heaven, but they reject both because, as they say, that they are against human nature. They do this in spite of those instances of heavenly goodness among them, which they honor as much as we do, and admire even more, since these things are not so difficult with us as with them. They fancy that goodness, and gentleness, and unselfishness, would somehow lose their value if they were the rule and not the exception, that they would become cheap in becoming common. Perhaps I can best make you understand all this by an illustration drawn from the æsthetic aspect of this vast city, which, I suppose is upon the whole, the ugliest city in the world. Ugliness is the rule in the architecture, which is for far the greatest part not merely ignoble and mean but positively offensive, insulting the eye by every conceivable or inconceivable stupidity and vulgarity of form. But in the midst of the chaotic ugliness there is from time to time, and from space to space, a beautiful edifice erected by some artist who has been able so far to circumvent some millionaire as to turn his money to that effect. I could instance half a score of exquisite masterpieces of this sort, but you would not be the wiser for my doing so. It is in architecture more than in any other art that the Americans have shown themselves gifted, but they have not shown it to such effect as to characterize their richest and greatest city with architectural beauty. On the contrary, so far from redeeming their environment, these gracious structures are lost and annulled in it. Your pleasure in them is spoiled by the sight of some monstrosity next to them, or by the sea of hideous forms that welters round them and overwhelms them from every side. They do not stand out from the sordid mass; they sink into it and leave you thinking of that, and bruised and quivering from the affront and hurt of it.

Commend me lovingly to all the Altrurians, and believe me, dear Cyril, most affectionately and constantly,

Your friend,
ARISTIDES HOMOS.

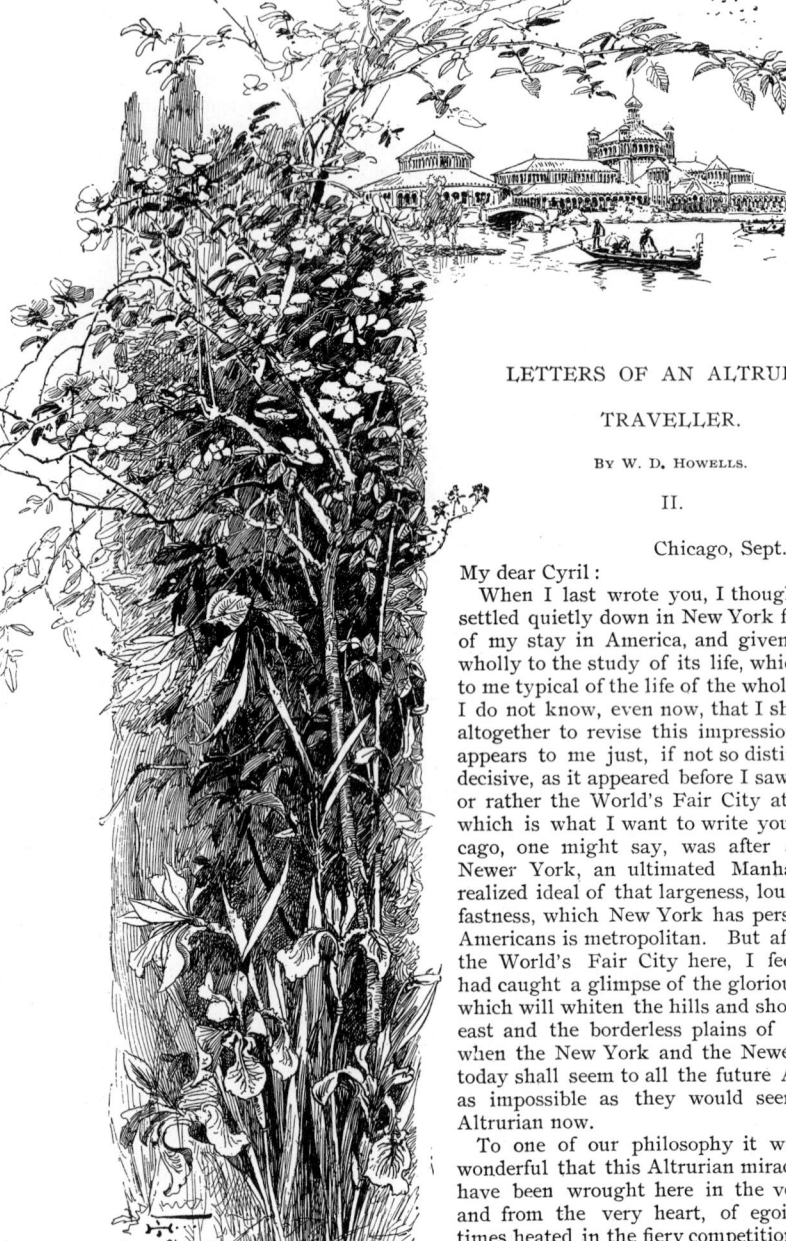

LETTERS OF AN ALTRURIAN TRAVELLER.

BY W. D. HOWELLS.

II.

Chicago, Sept. 28, 1893.

My dear Cyril:

When I last wrote you, I thought to have settled quietly down in New York for the rest of my stay in America, and given my time wholly to the study of its life, which seemed to me typical of the life of the whole country. I do not know, even now, that I should wish altogether to revise this impression; it still appears to me just, if not so distinct and so decisive, as it appeared before I saw Chicago, or rather the World's Fair City at Chicago, which is what I want to write you of. Chicago, one might say, was after all only a Newer York, an ultimated Manhattan, the realized ideal of that largeness, loudness and fastness, which New York has persuaded the Americans is metropolitan. But after seeing the World's Fair City here, I feel as if I had caught a glimpse of the glorious capitals which will whiten the hills and shores of the east and the borderless plains of the west, when the New York and the Newer York of today shall seem to all the future Americans as impossible as they would seem to any Altrurian now.

To one of our philosophy it will not be wonderful that this Altrurian miracle should have been wrought here in the very heart, and from the very heart, of egoism seven times heated in the fiery competition hitherto the sole joy of this strange people. We know that like produces like only up to a certain point, and that then unlike comes of like since all things are of one essence ; that from life comes death at last, and from death comes life again in the final issue. Yet it would be useless trying to persuade most Americans that the World's Fair City was not the effect, the fine flower, of the competition which underlies their economy, but was the first fruits of the principle of emulation which animates our happy commonwealth, and gives men, as no where else on earth, a foretaste of heaven. If I were writing to an American I should have to supply him with proofs and argue facts at every moment, which will be self-evident to you in their mere statement.

I confess that I was very loth to leave New York, which I fancied I was beginning to see whole, after my first fragmentary glimpses of it. But I perceive now that without a sight of the White City (as the Americans with their instant poetry called the official group of edifices at the great Fair) and the knowledge of its history, which I could have realized nowhere but in its presence, New York would have wanted the relief, the projection, in which I shall hereafter be able to study it. For the worst effect of sojourn in an egoistic civilization (I always use this word for lack of a closer descriptive) is that Altrurian motives and efforts become incredible, and almost inconceivable. But the Fair City is a bit of Altruria : it is as if the capital of one of our Regions had set sail and landed somehow on the shores of the vast inland sea, where the Fair City lifts its domes and columns.

Its story, which I need not rehearse to you at any length, records the first great triumph of Altrurian principles among this people in a work of peace ; in their mighty civil war they were Altrurian enough ; and more than once they have proved themselves capable of a magnificent self-sacrifice in bloodshed, but here for the first time in their pitiless economic struggle, their habitual warfare in which they neither give nor ask quarter, and take no prisoners, the interests submitted to the arts, and lent themselves as frankly to the work as if there had never been a question of money in the world. From the beginning it was believed that there could be no profit in the Fair; money loss was expected and accepted as a necessary part of the greater gain ; and when the question passed from how much to how, in the discussion of the ways and means of creating that beauty which is the supreme use, the capitalists put themselves into the hands of the artists. They did not do it at once, and they did not all do it willingly. It is a curious trait of the American who has made money that he thinks he can make anything ; and the Chicago millionaires who found themselves authorized by the nation to spend their money in the creation of the greatest marvel of the competitive world, thought themselves fully competent to work the miracle, or to choose the men who would work it according to their ideals. But their clarification, if it was not as swift as the passage of light was thorough, and I do not suppose there is now any group of rich men in Europe or America who have so luminous a sense of the true relations of the arts and the interests as they. The notion of a competition among the artists, which is the practical American's notion of the way to get the best art, was at length rejected by these most practical Americans, and one mind large enough to conceive the true means and strong enough to give its conception effect was empowered to invite the free coöperation of the arts through

Exhibit of the Fisheries and Japanese Tea-house, Chicago.

the foremost artists of the country. As yet the governmental function is so weak here that the national part in the work was chiefly obstructive, and finally null; and when it came to this there remained an opportunity for the arts, unlimited as to means and unhampered by conditions.

For the different buildings to be erected, different architects were chosen; and for the first time since the great ages, since the beauty of antiquity and the elegance of the renaissance, the arts were reunited. The greatest landscape gardeners, architects, sculptors and painters, gathered at Chicago for a joyous interchange of ideas and criticisms; and the miracle of beauty which they have wrought grew openly in their breath and under their hands. Each did his work and had his way with it, but in this congress of gifted minds, of sensitive spirits, each profited by the censure of all, and there were certain features of the work—as for instance, the exquisite peristyle dividing the city from the lake—which were the result of successive impulses and suggestions from so many different artists that it would be hard to divide the honor among them with exactness. No one, however, seems to have been envious of another's share, and each one gave his talent as freely as the millionaires gave their money. These great artists willingly accepted a fifth, a tenth, of the gain which they could have commanded in a private enterprise, and lavished their time upon the opportunity afforded them, for the pleasure of it, the pride of it, the pure good of it.

Of the effect, of the visible, tangible result, what better can I say, than that in its presence I felt myself again in Altruria? The tears came, and the pillared porches swam against my vision; through the hard nasal American tones, the liquid notes of our own speech stole to my inner ear; I saw under the careworn masks of the competitive crowds, the peace, the *rest* of the dear Altrurian face; the gay tints of our own simple costumes eclipsed the different versions of the Paris fashions about me. I was at home once more, and my heart overflowed with patriotic rapture in this strange land, so remote from ours in everything, that at times Altruria really seems to me the dream which the Americans think it.

I first saw the Fair City by night, from one of the electric launches which ply upon the lagoon; and under the dimmed heaven, in the splendor of the hundred moony arc-lamps of the esplanades, and the myriad incandescent bubbles that beaded the white quays, and defined the structural lines of dome and porch and pediment, I found myself in the midst of the Court of Honor, which you will recognize on the general plan and the photographs I enclose. We fronted the beautiful Agricultural building, which I think fitly the finest in the city, though many prefer the perfect Greek of the Art building; and on our right was the Administration building with its coroneted dome, and the magnificent sculptured fountain before it, turned silver in the radiance of the clustered electric jets at either side. On our right was the glorious peristyle, serene, pure, silent, lifting a population of statues against the night, and dividing the lagoon from the lake, whose soft moan came appealingly through the pillared spaces, and added a divine heartache to my ecstacy. Here a group of statuary showed itself prominently on quay or cornice; we caught the flamy curve of a bridge's arch; a pale column lifted its jutting prores into the light; but nothing insisted; all was harmonized to one effect of beauty, as if in symbol of the concentered impulses which had created it. For the moment I could not believe that so foul a thing as money could have been even the means of its creation. I call the effect creation because it is divinely beautiful, but no doubt suggestion would be a better word, since they have here merely sketched in stucco what we have executed in marble in each of our Regionic capitals.

In grandeur of design and freedom of expression, it is perhaps even nobler than the public edifices of some of these, as I had to acknowledge at another moment, when we rounded the shores of the Wooded Island which forms the heart of the lagoon, and the launch slowed while we got the effect of its black foliage against the vast lateral expanse of the Liberal Arts building. Then, indeed, I was reminded of our national capitol, when it shows its mighty mass above the bosks around it, on some anniversary night of our Evolution.

But the illusion of Altruria was very vivid at many moments in the Fair City, where I have spent the happiest days of my stay in America, perhaps because the place is so little American in the accepted sense. It is like our own cities in being a design, the effect of a principle, and not the straggling and shapeless accretion of accident. You will see, from the charts and views I send you, something of the design in detail, but you can form only a dim conception of the skill with which the natural advantages of the site have been turned to account, and even its disadvantages have been transmuted to the beauty which is the highest and last result of all. There was not only the great lake here, which contributes so greatly to this beauty, but there were marshes to be drained and dredged before its pure waters could be invited in. The trees which at different points offer the contrast of their foliage to the white of the edifices, remain from wilding growths which overspread the swamps and sand dunes, and which had to be destroyed in great part before these lovely groves could be evoked from them. The earth itself, which now of all the earth seems the spot best adapted to the site of such a city, had literally to be formed anew for the use it has been put to. There is now no shadow, no hint of the gigantic difficulties of the undertaking, which was carried on in the true Altrurian spirit, so far as the capitalists and artists were concerned, and with a joy like ours in seeing nature yield herself to the enlightened will of man. If I told you how time itself was overcome in this work by the swiftness of modern methods, it would be nothing new to you, for we are used to seeing the powerful machinery of our engineers change the face of the landscape, without stay for the slow processes of other days, when the ax and the saw wrought for years in the destruction of the forests that now vanish in a night. But to the Americans these things are still novel, and they boast of the speed with which the trees were dragged from the soil where they were rooted, and the morasses were effaced, and the wastes of sand made to smile with the verdure that now forms the most enchanting feature of their normal city.

They dwell upon this, and they do not seem to feel as I do the exquisite simplicity with which its life is operated, the perfection with which it is policed, and the thoroughness with which it has been dedicated to health as well as beauty. In

A BIT OF THE GERMAN BUILDING.

fact, I fancy that very few out of the millions who visit this gala town realize that it has its own system of drainage, lighting and transportation, and its own government, which looks as scrupulously to the general comfort and cleanliness, as if these were the private concern of each member of the government. This is, as it is with us, military in form, and the same precision and discipline which give us the ease and freedom of our civic life, proceed here from the same spirit and the same means. The Columbian Guards, as they are called, who are here at every turn, to keep order and to care for the pleasure as well as the welfare of the people, have been trained by officers of the United States army, who still command them, and they are amenable to the rules governing the only body in America whose ideal is not interest but duty. Every night, the whole place is cleansed of the rubbish which the visitors leave behind them, as thoroughly as if it were a camp. It is merely the litter of lunch-boxes and waste paper which has to be looked after, for there is little of the filth resulting in all other American cities from the use of the horse, which is still employed in them so many centuries after it has been banished from ours. The United States mail-carts and the watering-carts are indeed anomalously drawn through the Fair City thoroughfares by horses, but wheeled chairs pushed about by a corps of high school boys and college undergraduates form the means of transportation by land for those who do not choose to walk. On the water, the electric launches are quite of our own pattern, and steam is allowed only on the boats which carry people out into the lake for a view of the peristyle. But you can get this by walking, and as in Venice, which is represented here by a fleet of gondolas, there are bridges that enable you to reach every desirable point on the lagoon.

When I have spoken of all this to my American friends they have not perceived the moral value of it, and when I have insisted upon the practical perfection of the scheme apparent in the whole, they have admitted it, but answered me that it would never do for a business city, where there was something going on besides the pleasure of the eyes and the edification of the mind. When I tell them that this is all that our Altrurian cities are for, they do not understand me; they ask where the money is made that the people live on in such play-cities; and we are alike driven to despair when I try to explain that we have no money, and should think it futile and impious to have any.

I do not believe they quite appreciate the intelligence with which the Fair City proper has been separated, with a view to its value as an object lesson, from all the state and national buildings in the ground. Some of the national buildings, notably those of Germany and Sweden, are very picturesque, but the rest decline through various grades of inferiority, down to the level of the State buildings. Of these, only the California and the New York buildings have a beauty comparable to that of the Fair City: the California house, as a reminiscence of the Spanish ecclesiastical architecture in which her early history is recorded, and the New York house, as a sumptuous expression of the art which ministers to the luxury of the richest and greatest State of the Union

By still another remove the competitive life of the present epoch is relegated to the long avenue remotest from the White City, which you will find marked as the Midway Plaisance. Even this, where a hundred shows rival one another in a furious advertisement for the favor of the passer, there is so much of a high interest that I am somewhat loth to instance it as actuated by an inferior principle; and I do so only for the sake of the contrast. In the Fair City, everything is free; in the Plaisance everything must be paid for. You strike at once here the hard level of the outside western world; and the Orient, which has mainly peopled the Plaisance, with its theaters and restaurants and shops, takes the tint of the ordinary American enterprise, and puts on somewhat the manners of the ordinary American hustler. It is not really so bad as that, but it is worse than American in some of the appeals it makes to the American public, which is decent if it is dull, and respectable if it is rapacious. The lascivious dances of the East are here, in the Persian and Turkish and Egyptian theaters, as well as the exquisite archaic drama of the Javanese and the Chinese in their village and temple. One could spend many days in the Plaisance, always entertainingly, whether profitably or unprofitably; but whether one visited the Samoan or Dahomeyan in his hut, the Bedouin and the Lap in their camps; the delicate Javanese in his bamboo cottage, or the American Indian in his tepee, one must be aware that the citizens of the Plaisance are not there for their health, as the Americans quaintly say, but for the money there is in it. Some of the reproductions of historical and foreign scenes are excellent, like the irregular square of Old Vienna, with its quaintly built and quaintly decorated shops; the German village, with its admirably realized castle and chalet; and the Cairene street, with its motley oriental life; but these are all there for the profit to be had from the pleasure of their visitors, who seem to pay as freely as they talk through their noses. The great Ferris wheel itself, with its circle revolving by night and by day in an orbit incomparably vast, is in the last analysis a money-making contrivance.

I have tried to make my American friends see the difference, as I do, between the motive that created the Fair City, and the motive that created the Plaisance, but both seem to them alike the outcome of the principle which they still believe animates their whole life. They think both an effect of the competitive conditions in which they glory, not knowing that their conditions are now purely monopolistic, and not perceiving that the White City is the work of an armistice between the commercial interests ruling them. I expressed this belief to one of them, the banker, whom I met last summer in the country, and whom I ran upon one night during the first week of my visit here; and he said there could certainly be that view of it. But, like the rest, he asked where the money would have come from without the warfare of competitive conditions, and he said he could not make out how we got the money for our public works in Altruria, or, in fact, how we paid the piper. When I answered that as each one of us was secured by all against want, every one could freely give his labor, without money and without price, and the piper could play for the pure pleasure of playing, he looked stupefied and said incredulously, "Oh, come, now!"

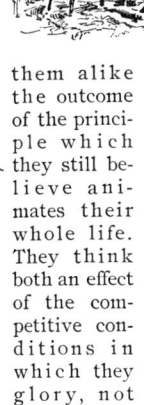

"Why, how strange you Americans are," I could not help breaking out upon him, "with your talk about competition! There *is* no competition among you a moment longer than you can help, a moment after one proves himself stronger than another. Then you have monopoly, which even upon the limited scale it exists here is the only vital and fruitful principle, as you all see. And yet you are afraid to have it upon the largest possible scale,

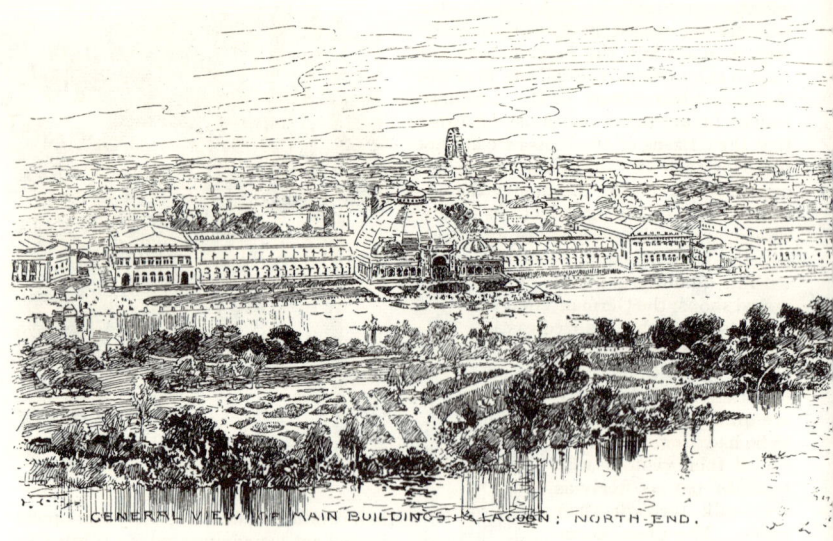
GENERAL VIEW OF MAIN BUILDINGS & LAGOON; NORTH END.

the national scale, the scale commensurate with the whole body politic, which implicates care for every citizen as the liege of the collectivity. When you have monopoly of such proportions money will cease to have any office among you, and such a beautiful creation as this will have effect from a consensus of the common wills and wishes."

He listened patiently, and he answered amiably, "Yes, that is what you Altrurians believe, I suppose, and certainly what you preach; and if you look at it in that light, why there certainly is no competition left, except between the monopolies. But you must allow, my dear Homos," he went on, "that at least one of the twin fetishes of our barbarous worship has had something to do with the creation of all this beauty. I'll own that you have rather knocked the notion of competition on the head; the money that made this thing possible never came from competition at all; it came from some sort or shape of monopoly, as all money always does; but what do you say about individuality? You can't say that individuality has had nothing to do with it. In fact, you can't deny that it has had everything to do with it, from the individuality of the several capitalists, up or down, to the individuality of the several artists. And will you pretend in the face of all this wonderful work that individuality is a bad thing?"

"Have I misrepresented myself and country so fatally," I returned, "as to have led you to suppose that the Altrurians thought individuality a bad thing? It seems to us the most precious gift of the Deity, the dearest and holiest possession of his creatures. What I lament in America at every moment, what I lament even here, in the presence of a work so largely Altrurian in conception and execution as this, is the wholesale effacement, the heartbreaking obliteration of individuality. I know very well that you can give me the name of the munificent millionaires—large-thoughted and noble-willed men—whose largesse made this splendor possible, and the name of every artist they freed to such a glorious opportunity. Their individuality is lastingly safe in your memories; but what of the artisans of every kind and degree, whose patience and skill realized their ideals? Where will you find *their* names?"

My companions listened respectfully, but not very seriously, and in his reply he took refuge in that humor peculiar to the Americans: a sort of ether where they may draw breath for a moment free from the stifling despair which must fill every true man among them when he thinks how far short of their ideal their reality has fallen.

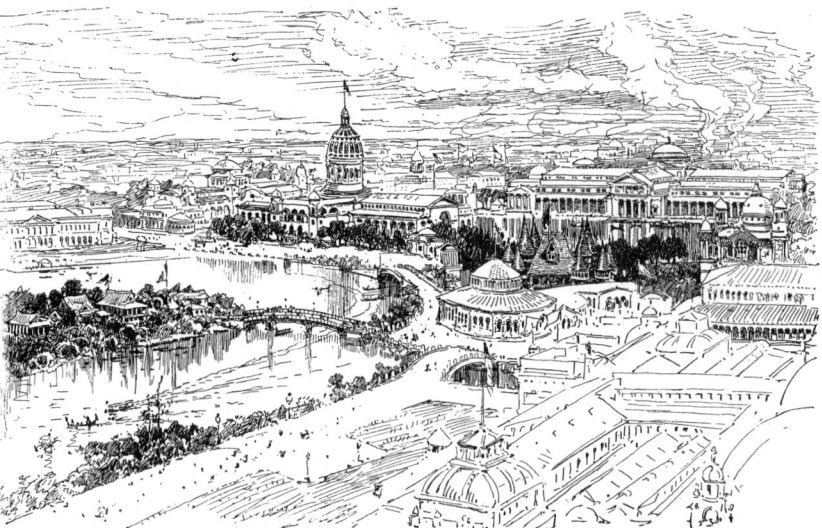

For they were once a people with the noblest ideal; we were not mistaken about that; they did, indeed, intend the greatest good to the greatest number, and not merely the largest purse to the longest head. They are a proud people, and it is hard for them to confess that they have wandered from the right way, and fallen into a limitless bog, where they can only bemire themselves more and more till its miasms choke them or its foul waters close over them.

"My dear fellow," the banker laughed, "you are very easily answered. You will find *their* names on the pay-rolls, where, I've no doubt, they preferred to have them. Why, there was an army of them; and we don't erect monuments to private soldiers, except in the lump. How would you have managed it in Altruria?"

"In Altruria," I replied, "every man who drove a nail, or stretched a line, or laid a trowel upon such a work, would have had his name somehow inscribed upon it, where he could find it, and point it out to those dear to him and proud of him. Individuality! I find no record of it here, unless it is the individuality of the few. That of the many makes no sign from the oblivion in which it is lost, either in these public works of artistic coöperation, or the exhibits of your monopolistic competition. I have wandered through these vast edifices and looked for the names of the men who wrought the marvels of ingenuity that fill them. But I have not often found the name even of a man who owns them. I have found the styles of the firms, the companies, the trusts which turn them out as impersonally as if no heart had ever ached or glowed in imagining and embodying them. This whole mighty industrial display is in so far dehumanized; and yet you talk of individuality as one of your animating principles!"

"You are hopelessly unbusinesslike, my dear Homos," said the banker, "but I like your unpracticability. There is something charming in it; there is, really; and I enjoy it particularly at this moment because it has enabled me to get back my superiority to Chicago. I am a Bostonian, you know, and I came out here with all the misgivings which a Bostonian begins to secrete as soon as he gets west of the Back Bay Fens. It is a survival of Puritanism in us. In the old times, you know, every Bostonian, no matter how he prayed and professed, felt it in his bones that he was one of the elect, and we each feel so still; only, then God elected us, and now we elect ourselves. Fancy such a man confronted with such an achievement as this, and unfriended yet by an Altrurian traveller!

Why, I have gone about the last three days inwardly bowed down before Chicago in the most humiliating fashion. I've said to myself that our eastern fellows did half the thing, perhaps the best half; but then I had to own it was Chicago that imagined letting them do it, that imagined the thing as a whole, and I had to give Chicago the glory. When I looked at it I had to forgive Chicago Chicago, but now that you've set me right about the matter, and I see that the whole thing is dehumanized, I shall feel quite easy, and I shall not give Chicago any more credit than is due."

I saw that he was joking, but I did not see how far, and I thought it best not to take him in joke at all. "Ah, I don't think you can give her too much credit, even if you take her at the worst. It seems to me, from what I have seen of your country—and, of course, I speak from a foreigner's knowledge only — that no other American city could have brought this to pass."

"You must come and stay with us a while in Boston," said the banker; and he smiled. "One other city could have done it. Boston has the public spirit and Boston has the money, but perhaps Boston has not the ambition. Perhaps we give ourselves in Boston too much to a sense of the accomplished fact. If that is a fault, it is the only fault conceivable of us. Here in Chicago they have the public spirit, and they have the money, and they are still anxious to do; they are not content as we are, simply to be. Of course, they have not so much reason! I don't know," he added thoughtfully, "but it comes in the end to what you were saying, and no other American city but Chicago *could* have brought this to pass. Leaving everything else out of the question, I doubt if any other community could have fancied the thing in its vastness; and the vastness seems an essential condition of the beauty. You couldn't possibly say it was pretty, for instance; if you admitted it was fine you would have to say it was beautiful. To be sure, if it were possible to have too much of a good thing, there are certain states of one's legs, here, when one could say there was too much of it; but that is not possible. But come, now; be honest for once, my dear fellow, and confess that you really prefer the Midway Plaisance to the Fair City!"

I looked at him with silent reproach, and he broke out laughing, and took me by the arm.

"At any rate," he said, "let us go down there, and get something to eat.

'The glory that was Greece,
And the grandeur that was Rome,'

here, take it out of you so that I find myself wanting lunch about every three hours. It's nearly as long as that now, since I dined, and I feel an irresistible yearning for Old Vienna, where that pinchbeck halberdier of a watchman is just now crying the hour of nine."

"Oh, is it so late as that?" I began, for I like to keep our Altrurian hours even here, when I can, and I was going to say that I could not go with him when he continued:

"They won't turn us out, if that's what you mean. Theoretically, they do turn people out toward the small hours, but practically, one can stay here all night, I believe. That's a charming thing about the Fair, and I suppose it's rather Chicagoan; if we'd had the Fair in Boston, every soul would have had to leave before midnight. We couldn't have helped turning them out, from the mere oldmaidishness of our Puritanic tradition, and not because we really minded their staying. In New York they would have put them out from Keltic imperiousness, and locked them up in the station-house when they got them out, especially if they were sober and inoffensive."

I could not follow him in this very well, or in the playful allusiveness of his talk generally, though I have reported it, to give some notion of his manner; and so I said, by way of bringing him within easy range of my intelligence again, "I have seen no one here who showed signs of drink."

"No," he returned. "What a serious, and peaceable, and gentle crowd it is! I haven't witnessed a rudeness, or even an unkindness, since I've been here, and nobody looks as if anything stronger than apollinaris had passed his lips for a fortnight. They seem, the vast majority of them, to pass their time in the Fair City, and I wish I could flatter myself that they preferred it, as you wish me to think you do, to the Plaisance. Perhaps they are really more interested in the mechanical arts, and even the fine arts, than they are in the muscle dances, but I'm afraid it's partly because there isn't an additional charge for admission to those improving exhibits in the official buildings. Though I dare say that most of the hardhanded folks here, are really concerned in transportation and agricultural implements to a degree that it is difficult for their more cultivated fellow-countrymen to conceive of. Then, the merely instructive and historical features must have an incredible lot to say to them. We people who have had advantages, as we call them, can't begin to understand the state that most of us come here in, the state of enlightened ignorance, as one may call it, when we know how little we know, and are anxious to know more. But I congratulate you, Homos, on the opportunity you have to learn America personally, here; you won't easily have such another chance. I'm glad for your sake, too, that it (the crowd) is mainly a western and south-western crowd, a Mississippi Valley crowd. You can tell it by their accent. It's a mistake to suppose that New England has a monopoly of the habit of speaking through the nose. We may have invented it, but we have imparted it apparently to the whole west, as the Scotch-Irish of Pennsylvania have lent the twist of their "r," and the combined result is something frightful. But it's the only frightful thing about the westerners, as I find them here. Their fashions are not the latest, but they are not only well behaved, they are on the average pretty well dressed, as the clothing store and the paper pattern dress our people. And they look pathetically good! When I think how hard-worked they all are, and what lonely lives most of them live on their solitary farms, I wonder they don't descend upon me with the whoop of savages. You're very fond of equality, my dear Homos! How do you like the equality of the American effect here? It's a vast level, as unbroken as the plains that seemed to widen as I came over them in the cars to Chicago, and that go widening on, I suppose, to the sunset itself. I won't speak of the people, but I *will* say the plains were dreary."

"Yes," I assented, for those plains had made me melancholy, too. They looked so habitable, and they were so solitary, though I could see that they were broken by the lines of cultivated fields, which were being plowed for wheat, or were left standing with their interminable ranks of maize. From time to time one caught sight of a forlorn farmstead, with a windmill beside it, making helpless play with its vanes as if it were vainly struggling to take flight from the monotonous landscape. There was nothing of the cheerfulness of our Altrurian farm villages; and I could understand how a dull uniformity of the human type might result from such an environment, as the banker intimated.

I have made some attempts, here, to get upon speaking terms with these average people, but I have not found them

In the Turkish quarters

conversible. Very likely they distrusted my advances, from the warnings given them to beware of imposters and thieves at the Fair; it is one of the necessities of daily life in a competitive civilization, that you must be on your guard against strangers lest they cheat or rob you. It is hard for me to understand this, coming from a land where there is no theft and can be none, because there is no private property, and I have often bruised myself to no purpose in attempting the acquaintance of my fellow-visitors of the Fair. They never make any attempt at mine; no one has asked me a favor, here, or even a question; but each remains bent, in an intense preoccupation, upon seeing the most he can in the shortest time for the least money. Of course, there are many of the more cultivated visitors, who are more responsive, and who show themselves at least interested in me as a fellow-stranger; but these, though they are positively many, are, after all, relatively few. The vast bulk, the massed members of that immense equality which fatigued my friend, the banker, by its mere aspect, were shy of me, and I do not feel that I came to know any of them personally. They strolled singly, or in pairs, or by family groups, up and down the streets of the Fair City, or the noisy thoroughfare of the Plaisance, or through the different buildings, quiescent, patient, inoffensive, but reserved and inapproachable, as far as I was concerned. If they wished to know anything they asked the guards, who never failed in their duty of answering them fully and pleasantly.

The people from the different states visited their several State buildings, and seemed to be at home, there, with that instinctive sense of ownership which every one feels in a public edifice, and which is never tainted with the greedy wish to keep others out. They sat in long rows on the benches that lined the avenues, munching the victuals they had mostly brought with them in the lunch-boxes which strewed the place at nightfall, and were gathered up by thousands in the policing of the grounds. If they were very luxurious, they went to the tables of those eating-houses where, if they ordered a cup of tea or coffee, they could spread out the repast from their boxes and enjoy it more at their ease. But in none of these places did I see any hilarity in them, and whether they thought it unseemly or not to show any gayety, they showed none. They were peacefully content within the limits of their equality, and where it ended, as from time to time it must, they betrayed no discontent. That is what always astonishes me in America. The man of the harder lot accepts it unmurmuringly and with no apparent sense of injustice in the easier lot of another. He suffers himself, without a word, to be worse housed, worse clad, worse fed, than his merely luckier brother, who could give him no reason for his better fortune that an Altrurian would hold valid. Here, at the Fair, for example, on the days when the German village is open to the crowd without charge, the crowd streams through without an envious glance at the people dining richly and expensively at the restaurants, with no greater right than the others have to feed poorly and cheaply from their paper boxes. In the Plaisance, weary old farmwives and delicate women of the artisan class make way uncomplainingly for the ladies and gentlemen who can afford to hire wheeled chairs. As meekly and quietly they loiter by the shores of the lagoon and watch those who can pay to float upon their waters in the gondolas and electric launches. Everywhere the economic inequality is as passively accepted as if it were a

natural inequality, like difference in height or strength, or as if it were something of immemorial privilege, like birth and title in the feudal countries of Eu- rope. Yet, if one of these eco- nomically inferior Americans were told that he was not the peer of any and every other American, he would resent it as the grossest insult, such is the power of the inveterate political illusion in which the nation has been bred.

The banker and I sat long over our supper, in the graveled court of Old Vienna, talking of these things, and enjoying a bottle of delicate Rhenish wine under the mild September moon, not quite put out of countenance by the electric lamps. The gay parties about us broke up one after another, till we were left almost alone, and the watchman in his mediæval dress, with a halberd in one hand, and a lantern in the other, came round to call the hour for the last time. Then my friend beckoned to the waiter for the account, and while the man stood figuring it up, the banker said to me: "Well, you must come to Boston a hundred years hence, to the next Columbian Fair, and we will show you everybody trundled about and fed at the public expense. I suppose that's what you would like to see?"

"It is what we always see in Altruria," I answered. "I haven't the least doubt it will be so with you in much less than a hundred years."

The banker was looking at the account the waiter handed him. He broke into an absent laugh, and then said to me, "I beg your pardon! You were saying?"

"Oh, nothing," I answered, and then, as he took out his pocket-book to pay, he laid the bill on the table, and I could not help seeing what our little supper had cost him. It was twelve dollars; and I was breathless; it seemed to me that two would have been richly enough.

"They give you a good meal here, don't you think?" he said. "But the worst of having dined or supped well is reflecting that if you hadn't you could have given ten or twelve fellows, who will have to go to bed supperless, a handsome surfeit; that you could have bought twenty-five hungry men a full meal each; that you could have supplied forty-eight with plenty; that you could have relieved the famine of a hundred and twenty-four. But what is the use? If you think of these things you have no peace of your life!"

I could not help answering, "We don't have to think of them in Altruria."

"Ah, I dare say," answered the banker, as he tossed the waiter a dollar, and we rose and strolled out into the Plaisance. "If all men were unselfish, I should agree with you that Altrurianism was best."

"You can't have unselfishness till you have Altrurianism," I returned. "You can't put the cart before the horse."

"Oh, yes, we can," he returned in his tone of banter. "We always put the cart before the horse in America, so that the horse can see where the cart is going."

We strolled up and down the Plaisance, where the crowd had thinned to a few stragglers like ourselves. Most of the show villages were silenced for the night. The sob of the Javanese water-wheel was hushed; even the hubbub of the Chinese theater had ceased. The Samoans slept in their stucco huts; the Bedouins were

folded to slumber in their black tents. The great Ferris wheel hung motionless with its lamps like a planetary circle of fire in the sky. It was a moment that invited to musing, that made a tacit companionship precious. By an impulse to which my own feeling instantly responded, my friend passed his arm through mine.

"Don't let us go home at all! Let us go over and sleep in the peristyle. I have never slept in a peristyle, and I have a fancy for trying it. Now, don't tell me you always sleep in peristyles in Altruria!"

I answered that we did not habitually, at least, and he professed that this was some comfort to him; and then he went on to talk more seriously about the Fair, and the effect that it must have upon American civilization. He said that he hoped for an æsthetic effect from it, rather than any fresh impulse in material enterprise, which he thought the country did not need. It had inventions enough, millionaires enough, prosperity enough; the great mass of the people lived as well and travelled as swiftly as they could desire. Now what they needed was some standard of taste, and this was what the Fair City would give them. He thought that it would at once have a great influence upon architecture, and sober and refine the artists who were to house the people; and that one might expect to see everywhere a return to the simplicity and beauty of the classic forms, after so much mere wandering and maundering in design, without authority or authenticity.

I heartily agreed with him in condemning the most that had yet been done in architecture in America, but I tried to make him observe that the simplicity of Greek architecture came out of the simplicity of Greek life, and the preference given in the Greek state to the intellectual over the industrial, to art over business. I pointed out that until there was some enlightened municipal or national control of the matter, no excellence of example could avail, but that the classicism of the Fair City would become, among a wilful and undisciplined people, a fad with the rich and a folly with the poor, and not a real taste with either class. I explained how with us the state absolutely forbade any man to aggrieve or insult the rest by the exhibition of his ignorance in the exterior of his dwelling, and how finally architecture had become a government function, and fit dwellings were provided for all by artists who approved themselves to the public criticism. I ventured so far as to say that the whole competitive world, with the exception of a few artists, had indeed lost the sense of beauty, and I even added that the Americans as a people seemed never to have had it at all.

He was not offended, as I had feared he might be, but asked me with perfect good nature what I meant.

"Why, I mean that the Americans came into the world too late to have inherited that influence from the antique world which was lost even in Europe, when in mediæval times the picturesque barbarously substituted itself for the beautiful, and a feeling for the quaint grew up in place of love for the perfect."

"I don't understand, quite," he said, but I'm interested. Go on!"

"Why," I went on, "I have heard people rave over the beauty of the Fair City, and then go and rave over the beauty of the German village, or of Old Vienna, in the Plaisance. They were cultivated people, too; but they did not seem to know that the reproduction of a feudal castle or of a street in the taste of the middle ages, could not be beautiful, and could at the best be only picturesque. Old Vienna is no more beautiful than the Javanese village, and the German village outrivals the Samoan village only in its greater adaptability to the purposes of the painter. There is in your modern competitive world very little beauty anywhere, but there is an abundance of picturesqueness, of forms that may be reflected upon canvas, and impart the charm of their wild irregularity to all who look at the picture, though many who enjoy it there would fail of it in a study of the original. I will go so far as to say that there are points in New York, intrinsically so hideous that it makes me shudder to recall them—"

"*Don't* recall them!" he pleaded.

"Which would be much more capable of pictorial treatment than the Fair City, here," I continued. We had in fact got back to the Court of Honor, in the course of our talk, which I have only sketched here in the meagerest abstract. The incandescent lamps had been

A CORNER OF THE AGRICULTURAL BUILDING.

quenched, and the arc-lights below and the moon above flooded the place with one silver, and the absence of the crowds that had earlier thronged it, left it to a solitude indescribably solemn and sweet. In that light, it was like a ghost of the antique world witnessing a loveliness lost to modern times everywhere but in our own happy country.

I felt that silence would have been a fitter tribute to it than any words of mine, but my companion prompted me with an eager, "Well!" and I went on.

"This beauty that we see here is not at all picturesque. If a painter were to attempt to treat it picturesquely, he must abandon it in despair, because the charm of the picturesque is in irregularity, and the charm of the beautiful is in symmetry, in just proportion, in equality. You Americans do not see that the work of man, who is the crown of animate life, can only be beautiful as it approaches the regularity expressive of beauty in that life. Any breathing thing that wants perfect balance of form or feature is in so far ulgy; it is offensive and ridiculous, just as a perfectly balanced tree or hill would be. Nature is picturesque, but what man creates should be beautiful, or else it is inferior. Since the Greeks, no people have divined this but the Altrurians, until now; and I do not believe that you would have begun to guess at it as you certainly have here, but for the spread of our ideas among you, and I do not believe this example will have any lasting effect with you unless you become Altrurianized. The highest quality of beauty is a spiritual quality."

"I don't know precisely how far I have followed you," said my companion, who seemed struck by a novelty in truisms which are so trite with us, "but I certainly feel that there is something in what you say. You are probably right in your notion that the highest quality of beauty is a spiritual quality, and I should like very much to know what you think that spiritual quality is here."

"The quality of self-sacrifice in the capitalists who gave their money, and in the artists who gave their talent without hope of material return, but only for the pleasure of authorizing and creating beauty that shall last forever in the memory of those it has delighted."

The banker smiled compassionately. "Ah, my dear fellow, you must realize that this was only a spurt. It could be done once, but it couldn't be kept up."

"Why not?" I asked.

"Because people have got to live, even capitalists and artists have got to live, and they couldn't live by giving away wealth and giving away work, in our conditions."

"But you will change the conditions!"

"I doubt it," said the banker with another laugh. One of the Columbian guards passed near us, and faltered a little in his walk. "Do you want us to go out?" asked my friend.

"No," the young fellow hesitated. "Oh no!" and he continued his round.

"He hadn't the heart to turn us out." said the banker, "he would hate so to be turned out himself. I wonder what will become of all the poor fellows who are concerned in the government of the Fair City when they have to return to earth! It will be rough on them." He lifted his head, and cast one long look upon the miracle about us. "Good heavens!" he broke out, "And when they shut up shop, here, will all this beauty have to be destroyed, this fabric of a vision demolished? It would be infamous, it would be sacrilegious! I have heard some talk of their burning it, as the easiest way, the only way of getting rid of it. But it mustn't be, it can't be."

"No, it can't be," I responded fervently. "It may be rapt from sight in the flames like the prophet in his chariot of fire; but it will remain still in the hearts of your great people. An immortal principle, higher than use, higher even than beauty, is expressed in it, and the time will come when they will look back upon it, and recognize in it the first embodiment of the Altrurian idea among them, and will cherish it forever in their history, as the earliest achievement of a real civic life."

I believe this, my dear Cyril, and I leave it with you as my final word concerning the great Columbian Fair.

Yours in all brotherly affection,
A. HOMOS.

THE COSMOPOLITAN.

From every man according to his ability: to everyone according to his needs.

VOL. XVI.   JANUARY, 1894.   NO. 3.

LETTERS OF AN ALTRURIAN TRAVELLER.

BY W. D. HOWELLS.

A BIT OF ALTRURIA IN NEW YORK.

III.

New York, October 24, 1893.

WELL, my dear Cyril, I have returned to this Babylon, you see, from my fortnight's stay in that vision of Altruria at the great Fair in Chicago. I can, perhaps, give you some notion of the effect with me by saying that it is as if I were newly exiled and were exposing myself a second time to the shock of American conditions, stripped of the false hopes and romantic expectations which, in some sort, softened the impression at first. I knew what I had to look forward to when my eyes lost the last glimpse of the Fair City, and I confess that I had not much heart for it. If it had only been to arrive here, and at once take ship for home, I could have borne it; but I had denied myself this, in the interest of the studies of plutocratic civilization which I wish to make, and this purpose could not support me under the burden that weighed my spirits down. I had seen what might be, in the Fair City, and now I was to see again what the Americans say must be, in New York, and I shrank not only from the moral, but the physical ugliness of the thing.

But, in fact, do not the two kinds of ugliness go together? I asked myself the question as I looked about me in the ridiculous sleeping-car I had taken passage in from Chicago. Money had been lavished upon its appointments, as if it had been designed for the state progress of some barbarous prince through his dominions, instead of the conveyance of simple republican citizens from one place to another, on business. It was as expensively upholstered as the bad taste of its designer could contrive, and a rich carpet under foot caught and kept whatever disease-germs were thrown off by the slumbering occupant in their long journey; on the floor, at every seat, a silver-plated spittoon ministered to the filthy national habit. The interior was of costly foreign wood, which was everywhere covered with a foolish and meaningless carving; mirrors framed into the panels reflected the spendthrift absurdity through the whole length of the saloon. Of course, this waste in the equipment and decoration of the car meant the exclusion of the poorer sort of travellers, who were obliged to sit up all night in the day-cars, when they might have been lodged, for a fifth of what I paid, in a sleeping-car much more tasteful, wholesome and secure than mine, which was destined, sooner or later, in the furious risks of American travel, to be whirled over the side of an embankment, or plunged through a broken bridge, or telescoped in a collision, or piled in a heap of shattered and ruined splendors like its own, and consumed in a holocaust to the American god Hustle.

For not only are the comforts of travel here made so costly that none but the very well-to-do can afford them, but the service of the insufficiently manned trains and lines is overworked and underpaid. Even the poor negroes who make up the beds in the sleepers are scrimped of half a living by the companies which declare handsome dividends, and leave them to the charity of the fleeced and imperilled passengers. The Americans are peculiarly proud of their sleeping-car system, though I can hardly believe that when he is pinned into a broken seat, the most infatuated American can get much pleasure, while the flames advance swiftly upon him, out of the carving of the woodwork, or even the brass capitals of the onyx columns supporting nothing at either end of the car-roof. But until he is placed in some such predicament, the American hears with acquiescence, if not complacence, of the railroad slaughters which have brought the mortality of travel to and from the Fair during the past month up to a frightful sum. Naturally, if he does not mind the reports of these disasters, where his own name may any day appear in the list of killed or wounded, he is not vividly concerned in the fate of the thirty thousand trainmen who are annually mangled or massacred. He regards these dire statistics, apparently, as another proof of the immense activity of his country, and he does not stop, as he is hurled precariously over its continental spaces, and shot out of his train at his journey's end, from two to six hours late, to consider whether a public management of public affairs is not as well in economics as in politics.

I was fortunate in my journey to New York; I arrived only two hours behind time, and I arrived safe and sound. The Americans are quite satisfied with the large average of people who arrive safe and sound, in spite of the large numbers who do neither; and from time to time their newspapers print exultant articles to show how many get home in the full enjoyment of life and limb. I do not see that they celebrate so often the seasonable arrival of the surviving travellers, and, in fact, my experience of railroads in America is that the trains seldom bring me to my journey's end at the appointed hour. On each great through-road there is one very rapid train, which has precedence of all other travel and traffic, and which does arrive at the hour fixed; but the other trains, swift or slow, seem to come lagging in at all sorts of intervals after their schedule-time. If I instance my experience and observation of this fact, my friends are inclined to doubt it; and if I insist upon matching it with their own, they allege the irregularity of the government trains in Germany, without seeming to know more about them than they know of their own trains. They at once begin to talk largely of the celerity and frequency of these, and to express their wonder that the companies should come so near keeping their word to the public as they sometimes do.

However, I was thankful for my safety and my soundness, when I found myself again in New York, though I felt so loth to be here. If I could fitly have done so I would very willingly have turned and

Reproduced through the courtesy of J. S. Johnston.

taken the next train back to Chicago, since I must not take the next steamer on to Altruria. But if I had gone back, it could only have been for a fortnight more, since at the end of the month now so far spent, they must begin to destroy the beauty they have created in the Fair City there. I tried to console myself with this fact, but the sense of an irreparable loss, of banishment, of bereavement, remained with me for days, and is only now beginning to wear itself away into a kind of impersonal sorrow, and to blend with the bruise of my encounter with the brute ugliness of this place, which is none the less brute, because it is so often kindly. It is like the ugliness of some great unwieldy monster, which looks so helpless and so appealing, that you cannot quite abhor it, but experience a sort of compassion for its unloveliness. I had thought of it in that way at a distance, but when I came to see it again, I found that, even in this aspect it was hard to bear. So I came up from the station to this hotel where I am now lodged, and where my windows overlook the long reaches of the beautiful Central Park at such a height that unless I drop my glance, none of the shapeless bulks of the city intrude themselves between me and the effect of a vast forest. My hotel is itself one of the most preposterous of the structures which disfigure the city, if a city without a sky-line can be said to be disfigured by any particular structure. With several others as vast or as high, it forms a sort of gateway to the Park, from whose leafy depths, these edifices swaggering upward unnumbered stories, look like detached cliffs in some broken and jagged mountain range. They are built with savage disregard to one another, or to the other buildings about them, and with no purpose, apparently, but to get the most money out of the narrowest space of ground. Any objective sense of them is to the last degree painful, as any objective sense of the American life is, in its inequality and disproportion; but subjectively they are not so bad as that is, not so bad from the inside. At great cost they offer you an incomparable animal comfort, and they realize for the average American an ideal of princely magnificence, such as he has been instructed by all his traditions to regard as the chief good of success.

But for me the best thing about my hotel is that I can leave it when I will and descend to the level of the street below, where I can at once lose myself in woods as sweet and friendly as our groves at home, and wander through their aisles unmolested by the crowds that make them their resort so harmlessly that even the sylvan life there is unafraid. This morning, as I sat on a bench in one of the most frequented walks, I could almost have touched the sparrows on the sprays about me; a squirrel foraging for nuts, climbed on my knees, as if to explore my pockets. Of course, there is a policeman at every turn to see that no wrong is done these pretty creatures, and that no sort of trespass is committed by any in the domain of all; but I like to think that the security and immunity of the Park is proof of something besides the vigilance of its guardians; that it is a hint of a growing sense in the Americans that what is common is the personal charge of everyone in the community.

In the absence of the private interest here, I get back again to the Fair City, and the yet fairer cities of our own Altruria; and I hope that, if you cannot quite excuse my self-indulgence, in placing myself near the Park, you will at least be able to account for it. You must remember the perpetual homesickness gnawing at my heart, and you must realize how doubly strange an Altrurian finds himself in any country of the plutocratic world; and then, I think, you will understand why I spend, and even waste, so much of my time lingering in this lovely place. As I turn from my page and look out upon it, I see the domes and spires of its foliage beginning to feel the autumn and taking on those wonderful sunset tints of the American year in its decline; when I stray through its pleasant paths, I feel the pathos of the tender October air; but, better than these sensuous delights, in everything of it and in it, I imagine a prophecy of the truer state which I believe America is destined yet to see established. It cannot be that the countless thousands who continually visit it, and share equally in its beauty, can all come away insensible of the meaning of it; here and there someone must ask himself, and then ask others, why the whole of life should not be as generous and as just as this part of it; why he should not have a country as palpably his own as the Central Park is, where his ownership excludes the ownership of no other.

would wish to see conditions bettered so that they might not be confronted at every turn by the mere loathliness of poverty. But they likewise are the slaves of habit, and go the way the rich have gone since the beginning of time in those unhappy countries where there are rich and poor. Sometimes I think that as Shakespeare says of the living and the dead, the rich and the poor here are "but as pictures" to one another, without vital reality. It is only a luckless exile from Altruria like myself who sees them in their dreadful verity, and has a living sense of them; and I, too, lose this at times.

Sometimes I am glad to lose it, and this is why I would rather walk in the pathways of the Park than in the streets of the city, for the contrasts here are not so frequent, if they are glaring still. I do get away from them now and then, for a moment or two, and give myself wholly up to the delight of the place. It has been treated with an artistic sense which finds its best expression here, as with us, in the service of the community; but I do not think the Americans understand this, the civic spirit is so weak in them yet; and I doubt if the artists themselves are conscious of it, they are so rarely given the chance to serve the community. But somehow, when this chance offers, it finds the right man to profit by it, as in the system of parks at Chicago, the gardened spaces at Washington, and the Central Park in New York. Some of the decorative features here are bad, the sculpture is often foolish or worse, and the architecture is the outgrowth of a mood, where it is not merely peurile. The footways have been asphalted, and this is out of keeping with the rustic character of the place, but the whole design, and much of the detail in the treatment of the landscape, bears the stamp of a kindly and poetic genius. The Park is in nowise taken away from nature, but is rendered back to her, when all has been done to beautify

Some workman out of work, as he trudges aimlessly through its paths, must wonder why the city cannot minister to his need as well as his pleasure, and not hold aloof from him till he is thrown a pauper on its fitful charities. If it can give him this magnificent garden for his forced leisure, why cannot it give him a shop where he can earn his bread?

I may be mistaken. His thoughts may never take this turn at all. The poor are slaves of habit, they bear what they have borne, they suffer on from generation to generation, and seem to look for nothing different. But this is what I think for the poor people in the Park, not alone for the workman recently out of work, but for the workman so long out of it that he has rotted into one of the sodden tramps whom I meet now and then, looking like some forlorn wild beast, in the light of the autumnal leaves. That is the great trouble, here, my dear Cyril: you cannot anywhere get away from the misery of life. You would think that the rich for their own sakes

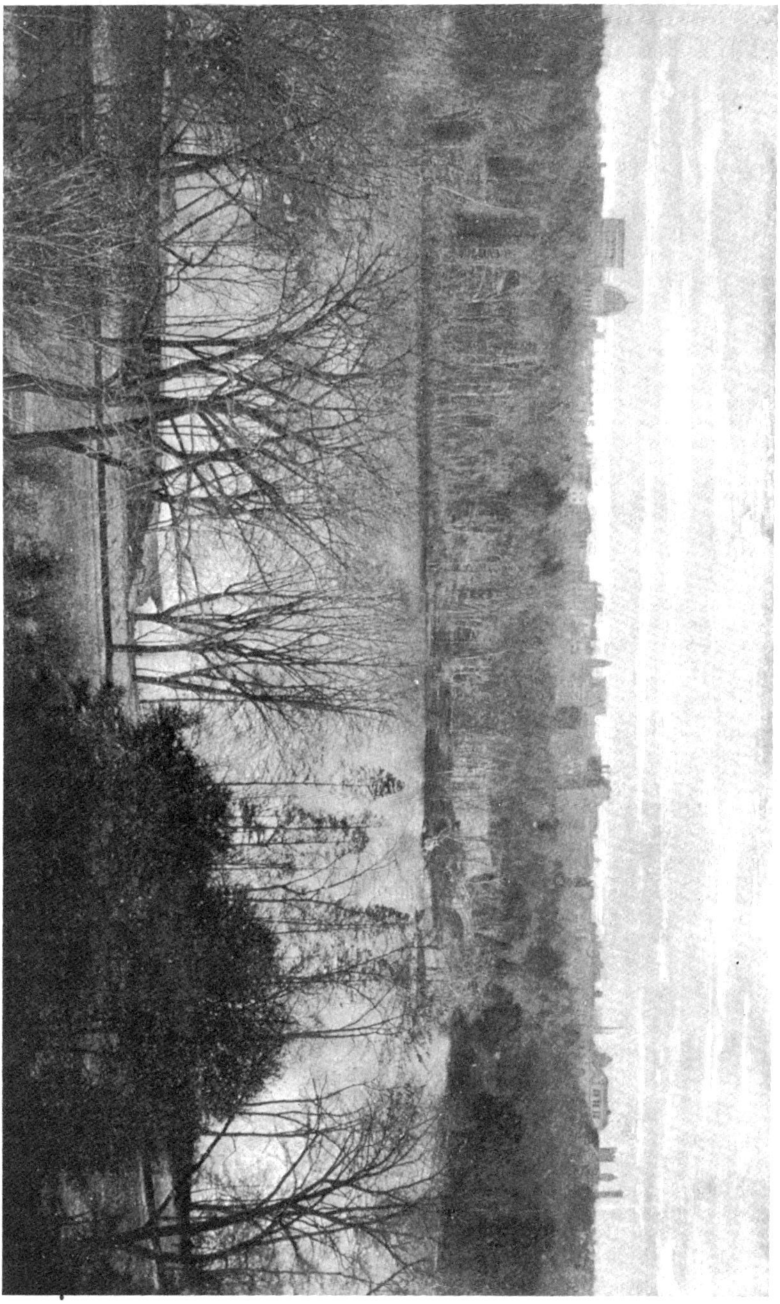

it, an American woodland, breaking into meadows, here and there, and brightened with pools and ponds lurking among rude masses of rock, and gleaming between leafy knolls and grassy levels. It stretches and widens away, mile after mile, in the heart of the city, a memory of the land as it was before the havoc of the city began, and giving to the city-prisoned poor an image of what the free country still is, everywhere. It is all penetrated by well-kept drives and paths; and it is in these paths that I find my pleasure. They are very simple woodland paths but for the asphalt; though here and there an effect of art is studied with charming felicity; once I mounted some steps graded in the rock, and came upon a plinth supporting the bust of a poet, as I might have done in our gardens at home. But there is otherwise very little effect of gardening except near the large fountain by the principal lake where there is some flare of flowers on the sloping lawns. I send you a photograph of this point, and you will see the excess of the viaduct, with its sweeping stairways, and carven freestone massiveness;—but it is charming in a way, too, and the basin of the fountain is full of lotoses and papyrus reeds, so that you do not much notice the bronze angel atop, who seems to be holding her skirt to one side and picking her steps, and to be rather afraid of falling into the water. There is, in fact, only one thoroughly good piece of sculpture in the Park, which I was glad to find in sympathy with the primeval suggestiveness of the landscape gardening: an American Indian hunting with his dog, as the Indians must have hunted through the wilds here before the white men came.

This group is always a great pleasure to me, from whatever point I come upon it, or catch a glimpse of it; and I like to go and find the dog's prototype in the wolves at the menagerie here which the city offers free to the wonder of the crowds constantly thronging its grounds and houses. The captive brutes seem to be of that solidarity of good fellowship which unites all the frequenters of the Park; the tigers and the stupidly majestic lions have an air different to me. at least, from tigers and lions shown for profit. Among the milder sorts, I do not care so much for the wallowing hippopotamuses, and the lumbering elephants, and the supercilious camels which one sees in menageries everywhere, as for those types which represent a period as extinct as that of the American pioneers: I have rather a preference for going and musing upon the ragged bison pair as they stand with their livid mouths open at the pale of their paddock, expecting the children's peanuts, and unconscious of their importance as survivors of the untold millions of their kind, which a quarter of a century ago blackened the western plains for miles and miles. There are now only some forty or fifty left; for of all the forces of the plutocratic conditions, so few are conservative that the American buffalo is as rare as the old-fashioned American mechanic, proud of his independence, and glorying in his citizenship.

In some other enclosures are pairs of the beautiful native deer, which I wish might be enlarged to the whole extent of the Park, as we have them in our Regionic parks at home. But I can only imagine them on the great sweeps of grass, which recall the savannahs and prairies, though there is a very satisfactory flock of sheep which nibbles the herbage there, when these spaces are not thrown open to the ball-players who are allowed on certain days of the week. I like to watch them, and so do great numbers of other frequenters of the Park, apparently; and when I have walked far up beyond the reservoirs of city-water, which serve the purpose of natural lakes in the landscape, I like to come upon that expanse in the heart of the woods where the tennis-players have stretched their nets over a score of courts, and the art students have set up their easels on the edges of the lawns, for what effect of the autumnal foliage they have the luck or the skill to get. It is all very sweet and friendly, and in keeping with the purpose of the Park, and its frank and simple treatment throughout.

From an Altrurian point of view I think this treatment is best for the greatest number of those who visit the place, and for whom the aspect of simple nature is the thing to be desired. Their pleasure in it, as far as the children are concerned, is visible and audible enough, but I like, as I stroll along, to note the quiet comfort which the elder people take in this domain of theirs, as they sit on the benches in the woodland ways, or under the arching trees of the Mall, unmolested by the company of some of the worst of all the bad statues in the plutocratic world. They are mostly foreigners, I believe, but I find every now and then an American among them, who has released himself, or has been forced by want of work, to share their leisure for the time ; I fancy he has always a bad conscience, if he is taking the time off, for there is a continual pressure of duty here, to add dollar to dollar, and provide for the future as well as the present need. The foreigner, who has been bred up without the American's hope of advancement, has not his anxiety, and is a happier man, so far as that goes ; but the Park imparts something of its peace to every one, even to some of the people who drive, and form a spectacle for those who walk.

For me they all unite to form a spectacle I never cease to marvel at, with a perpetual hunger of conjecture as to what they really think of one another. Apparently, they are all, whether they walk or whether they drive, willing collectively, if not individually, to go on forever in the economy which perpetuates their inequality, and makes a mock of the polity which assures them their liberty. I cannot get used to the difference which money creates among men here, and whenever I take my eyes from it the thing ceases to be credible ; yet this difference is what the vast majority of Americans have agreed to accept forever as right and justice. If I were to go and sit beside some poor man in the Park, and ask him why a man no better than he was driving before him in a luxurious carriage, he would say that the other man had the money to do it ; and he would really think he had given me a reason ; the man in the carriage himself could not regard the answer as more full and final than the man on the bench. They have both been reared in the belief that it is a sufficient answer, and they would both regard me with the same misgiving, if I ventured to say that it was not a reason ; for if their positions were to be at once reversed, they would both acquiesce in the moral outlawry of their inequality. The man on foot would think it had simply come his turn to drive in a carriage and the man whom he ousted would think it was rather hard luck, but he would realize that it was what, at the bottom of his heart, he had always expected.

I have sometimes ventured to address a man walking or sitting by my side, if he appeared more than commonly intelligent, in the hope of getting at some personal philosophy, instead of this conventional acceptance of the situation, but I have only had short or suspicious answers, or a bewildered stare for my pains. Only once have I happened to find any one who questioned the situation from a standpoint outside of it, and that was a shabbily dressed man whom I overheard talking to a poor woman in one of those pleasant arbors which crown certain points of rising ground in the Park. She had a paper bundle on the seat beside her, and she looked like some workingwoman out of place, with that hapless, wistful air, which such people often have. Her poor little hands, which lay in her lap, were stiffened and hardened with work, but they were clean, except for the black of the nails, and she was very decently clad in garments beginning to fray into rags; she had a good, kind, faithful face, and she listened without rancor to the man as he unfolded the truth to her concerning the conditions in which they lived, if it may be called living. It was the wisdom of the poor, hopeless, joyless, as it now and then makes itself heard in the process of the years and ages in the plutocratic world, and then sinks again into silence. He showed her how she had no permanent place in the economy, not because she had momentarily lost work, but because in the nature of things as the Americans have them, it could only be a question of time when she must be thrown out of any place she found. He blamed no one; he only blamed the conditions, and with far more leniency than you or I should. I do not know whether his wisdom made the friendless women happier, but I could not gainsay it, when he saw me listening, and asked me, "Isn't that the truth?" I left him talking sadly on, and I never saw him again. He looked very threadbare, but he too was cleanly and decent in his dress, and not at all of that type of agitators of whom the Americans have made an effigy like nothing I have ever found here, as if merely for the childish pleasure of reviling it.

The whole incident was infinitely pathetic to me; and yet I warn you, my dear Cyril, that you must not romance the poor, here, or imagine that they are morally better than the rich; you must not fancy that a poor man, when he ceases to be a poor man, would be kinder for having been poor. He would perhaps oftener, and certainly more logically, be unkinder, for there would be mixed with his vanity of possession a quality of cruel fear, an apprehension of loss, which the man who had always been rich would not feel. The self-made man in America, when he has made himself of money, seems to have been deformed by his original destitution, and I think that if I were in need I would rather take my chance of pity from the man who had never been poor. Of course, this is generalization, and there are instances to the contrary, which at once occur to me. But what is absolutely true, is that plutocratic prosperity, the selfish joy of having, at the necessary cost of those who cannot have, is blighted by the feeling of insecurity, which every man here has in his secret soul, and which the man who has known want must have in greater measure than the man who has never known want.

There is, indeed, no security for wealth, which the Americans think the chief good of life, in the system that warrants it. When a man has gathered his millions, he cannot be reduced to want, probably; but while he is amassing them, while he is in the midst of the fight, or the game, as most men are here, there are ninety-five chances out of a hundred that he will be beaten. Perhaps it is best so, and I should be glad it was so, if I could be sure that the common danger bred a common kindness between the rich and the poor here, but it seems not to do so. As far as I can see, the rule of chance, which they all live under, does nothing more than reduce them to a community of anxieties.

To the eye of the stranger they have the monotony of the sea, where some tenth wave runs a little higher than the rest, but sinks at last, or breaks upon the rocks or sands, as inevitably as the other nine. Their inequality is without picturesqueness and without distinction. The people in the carriages are better dressed than those on foot, especially the women; but otherwise they do not greatly differ from the most of these. The spectacle of the driving in the Park has none of that dignity which, our emissaries tell us, characterizes such spectacles in European capitals. This may be because many people of the finest social quality are still

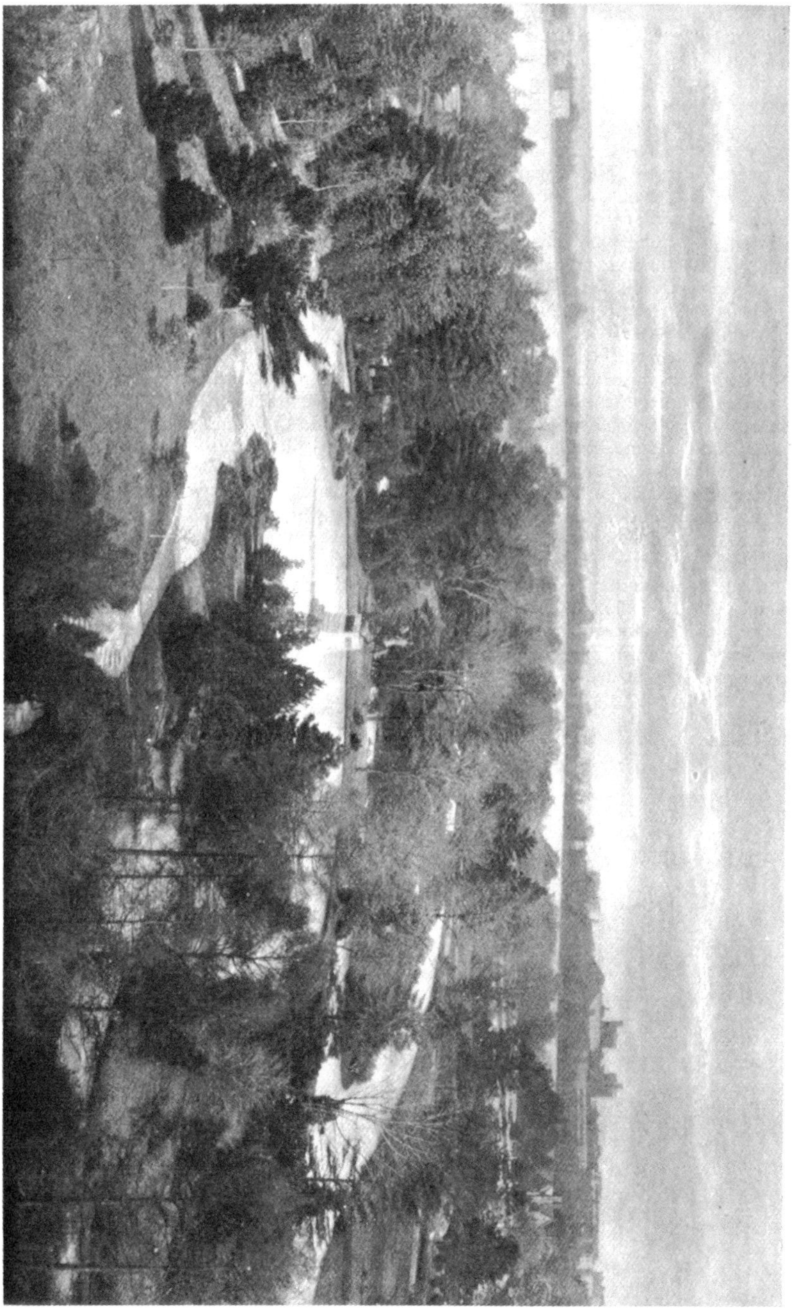

in the country, or it may be because the differences growing out of money can never have the effect of those growing out of birth; that a plutocracy can never have the last wicked grace of an aristocracy. It would be impossible, for instance, to weave any romance about the figures you see in the carriages here; they do not even suggest the poetry of ages of prescriptive wrong; they are of today, and there is no guessing whether they will be of tomorrow or not.

In Europe, this sort of tragicomedy is at least well played; but in America, you always have the feeling that the performance is that of second-rate amateurs, who, if they would really live out the life implied by America, would be the superiors of the whole world. I have, my dear Cyril, not a very keen sense of humor, as you know; but even I am sometimes moved to laughter by some of the things I see among them. Or, you perhaps think that I ought to be awed by the sight of a little, lavishly dressed lady, lolling in the corner of a ponderous landau, with the effect of holding fast lest she should be shaken out of it, while two powerful horses, in jingling, silver-plated harness, with the due equipment of coachman and footman, seated on their bright-buttoned overcoats on the box together, get her majestically over the ground at a slow trot. This is what I sometimes see, with not so much reverence as I feel for the simple mother pushing her baby-carriage on the asphalt beside me and doubtless envying the wonderful creature in the landau. Sometimes it is a fat old man in the landau; or a husband and wife, not speaking; or a pair of grim old ladies, who look as if they had lived so long aloof from their unluckier sisters that they could not be too severe with the mere sight of them. Generally speaking, the people in the carriages do not seem any happier for being there, though I have sometimes seen a jolly party of strangers in a public carriage, drawn by those broken-kneed horses which seem peculiarly devoted to this service.

The best place to see the driving is at a point where the different driveways converge, not far from the Egyptian obelisk which the Khedive gave the Americans some years ago, and which they have set up here in one of the finest eminences of the Park. He had of course no moral right to rob his miserable land of any one of its characteristic monuments, but I do not know that it is not as well in New York as in Alexandria. If its heart of aged stone could feel the terrible continuity of conditions in the world outside of Altruria, it must be aware of the essential unity of the civilizations beside the Nile and beside the Hudson ; and if Cleopatra's needle had really an eye to see, it must perceive that there is nothing truly civic in either. As the great tide of dissatisfied and weary wealth rolls by its base here, in the fantastic variety of its equipages, does it discern so much difference between their occupants and the occupants of the chariots that swept beneath it in the capital of the Ptolemies two thousand years ago? I can imagine it at times winking such an eye and cocking in derision the gilded cap with which the New Yorkers have lately crowned it. They pass it in all kinds of vehicles, and there are all kinds of people in them, though there are sometimes no people at all, as when the servants have been sent out to exercise the horses, for nobody's good or pleasure, and in the spirit of that atrocious waste which runs through the whole plutocratic life. I have now and then seen a gentleman driving a four-in-hand, with every- thing to minister to his vanity in the exact imitation of a nobleman driving a four-in-hand over English roads, and with no one to be drawn by his crop-tailed bays or blacks, except himself and the solemn-looking groom on his perch; I have wondered how much more nearly equal they were in their aspirations and instincts than either of them imagined. A gentleman driving a pair, abreast or tandem, with a groom on the rumble, for no purpose except to express his quality, is a common sight enough ; and sometimes you see a lady illustrating her consequence in like manner. A lady driving, while a gentleman occupies the seat behind her, is a sight which always affects me like the sight of a man taking a woman's arm, in walking, as the man of an underbred sort is apt to do here.

Horsey-looking women, who are, to ladies at least, what horsey-looking men are to gentlemen, drive together; often they are really ladies, and sometimes they are nice young girls, out for an innocent dash and chat. They are all very much and very unimpressively dressed, whether they sit in state behind the regulation coachman and footman, or handle the reins themselves. Now and then you see a lady with a dog on the seat beside her, for an airing, but not often a child; once or twice I have seen one with a large spaniel seated comfortably in front of her, and I have asked myself what would happen if, instead of the dog, she had taken into her carriage some pale woman or weary old man, such as I sometimes see gazing patiently after her. The thing would be possible in Altruria; but I assure you, my dear Cyril, it would be altogether impossible in America. I should be the first to feel the want of keeping in it; for, however recent wealth may be here, it has equipped itself with all the apparatus of long inherited riches, which it is as strongly bound to maintain intact as if it were really old and hereditary — perhaps more strongly. I must say that, mostly, its owners look very tired of it, or of something, in public, and that the American plutocrats, if they have not the distinction of an aristocracy, have at least the ennui.

But these stylish turnouts form only a part of the spectacle in the Park driveways, though they form, perhaps, the larger part. Bicyclers weave their dangerous and devious way everywhere through the roads, and seem to be forbidden the bridle-paths, where from point to point you catch a glimpse of the riders. There are boys and girls in village carts, the happiest of all the people you see; and there are cheap-looking buggies, like those you meet in the country here, with each a young man and young girl in them, as if they had come in from some remote suburb; turnouts shabbier yet, with poor old horses, poke about with some elderly pair, like a farmer and his wife. There are family carryalls, with friendly looking families, old and young, getting the good of the Park together in a long, leisurely jog; and open buggies with yellow wheels and raffish men in them behind their wide-spread trotters; or with some sharp-faced young fellow getting all the speed out of a lively span that the mounted policemen, stationed at intervals along the driveways, will allow. The finer vehicles are of all types, patterned like everything else that is fine in America, upon something fine in Europe; but just now a very high-backed phaeton appears to be most in favor; and in fact I get a great deal of pleasure out of these myself, as I do not have to sit stiffly up in them. They make me think somehow of those eighteenth-century English novels, which you and I used to delight in so much, and which filled us with a romantic curiosity concerning the times when young ladies like Evelina drove out in phaetons, and were the passionate pursuit of Lord Orvilles and Sir Clement Willoughbys.

You will be curious to know how far the Americans publicly carry their travesty of the European aristocratic life; and here I am somewhat at a loss, for I only know that life from the relations of our emissaries, and from the glimpses I had of it in my brief sojourn in England on my way here. But I should say, from what I have seen of the driving in the Park, where I suppose I have not yet seen the parody at its height, it does not err on the side of excess. The equipages, when they are fine, are rather simple ; and the liveries are such as express a proprietary grandeur in coat buttons, silver or gilt, and in a darker or lighter drab of the cloth the servants wear ; they are often in brown or dark green. Now and then you see the tightly cased legs and top boots and cockaded hat of a groom, but this is oftenest on a four-in-hand coach, or the rumble of a tandem cart ; the soul of the free-born republican is rarely bowed before it on the box of a family carriage. I have seen nothing like an attempt at family colors in the trappings of the coachman and horses.

Yes, I should say that the imitation was quite within the bounds of good taste. The bad taste is in the wish to imitate Europe at all ; but with the abundance of money, the imitation is simply inevitable. As I have told you before, and I cannot insist too much upon the fact, there is no American life for wealth ; there is no native formula for the expression of social superiority ; because America, like Altruria, means equality if it means anything, in the last analysis. But without economic equality there can be no social equality, and, finally, there can be no political equality ; for money corrupts the franchise, the legislature and the judiciary here, just as it used to do with us in the old days before the Evolution. Of all the American fatuities, none seems to me more deplorable than the pretension that with their conditions it can ever be otherwise, or that simple manhood can assert itself successfully in the face of such power as money wields over the very soul of man. At best, the common man can only break from time to time, into insolent defiance, pending his chance to make himself an uncommon man with money. In all this show here on the Park driveways, you get no effect so vivid as the effect of sterility in that liberty without equality which seems to satisfy the Americans. A man may come into the Park with any sort of vehicle, so that it is not for the carriage of merchandise, and he is free to spoil what might be a fine effect with the intrusion of whatever squalor of turnout he will. He has as much right there as any one, but the right to be shabby in the presence of people who are fine is not one that we should envy him. I do not think that he can be comfortable in it, for the superiority around him puts him to shame, as it puts the poor man to shame here at every turn in life, though some Americans, with an impudence that is pitiable, will tell you that it does not put him to shame ; that he feels himself as good as any one. They are always talking about human nature and what it is, and what it is not ; but they try in their blind worship of inequality, to refuse the first and simplest knowledge of human nature, which testifies of itself in every throb of their own hearts, as they try even to refuse a knowledge of the Divine nature, when they attribute to the Father of all a design in the injustice they have themselves created.

To me the lesson of Central Park is that where it is used in the spirit of fraternity and equality, the pleasure in it is pure and fine, and that its frequenters have for the moment a hint of the beauty which might be perpetually in their lives; but where it is invaded by the plutocratic motives of the strife that raves all round it in the city outside, its joys are fouled with contempt and envy, the worst passions that tear the human heart. Ninety-nine Americans out of a hundred, have never seen a man in livery; they have never dreamt of such a display as this in the Park; the sight of it would be as strange to them as it would be to all the Altrurians. Yet with their conditions, I fear that at sight of it, ninety-nine Americans out of every hundred, would lust for their turn of the wheel, their throw of the dice, so that they might succeed to a place in it, and flaunt their luxury in the face of poverty, and abash humility with their pride. They would not feel, as we should, the essential immorality of its deformity; they would not perceive that its ludicrous disproportion was the outward expression of an inward ugliness.

A. HOMOS.

THE ENTRANCE TO THE PARK FROM FIFTH AVENUE.

LETTERS OF AN ALTRURIAN TRAVELLER.

By W. D. Howells.

ASPECTS AND IMPRESSIONS OF A PLUTOCRATIC CITY.

IV.

New York, October 30, 1893.
My dear Cyril:

If you will look at a plan of New York, you will see that Central Park is really in the center of the place, if a thing which has length only, or is so nearly without breadth or thickness, can be said to have a center. South of the Park, the whole island is dense with life and business—it is pretty solidly built up on either side; but to the northward the blocks of houses are no longer of a compact succession; they struggle up, at irregular intervals, from open fields, and sink again, on the streets pushed beyond them into the simple country, where even a suburban character is lost. It can only be a few years, at most, before all the empty spaces will be occupied, and the town, such as it is, and such as it seems to have been ever since the colonial period, will have anchored itself fast in the rock that underlies the larger half of it, and imparted its peculiar effect to every street—an effect of arrogant untidiness, of superficial and formal gentility, of immediate neglect and overuse.

You will see more of the neglect and overuse in the avenues which penetrate the city's mass from north to south, and

"THE FRANTIC ACTIVITIES OF BUSINESS."

more of the superficial and formal gentility in the streets that cross these avenues from east to west; but the arrogant untidiness you will find nearly everywhere, except in some of the newest quarters westward from the Park, and still further uptown. These are really very clean; but they have a bare look, as if they were not yet inhabited, and, in fact, many of the houses are still empty. Lower down, the streets are often as shabby and as squalid as the avenues that run parallel with the river sides; and at least two of the avenues are as decent as the decentest cross-street. But all are more or less unkempt; the sweepings lie in little heaps in the gutters for days; and in a city without alleys barrels of ashes and kitchen offal line the curbstones and offer their offense to the nose and eye everywhere.

Of late, a good many streets and several avenues have been asphalted, and the din of wheels on the rough pavement no longer torments the ear so cruelly; but there is still the sharp clatter of the horses' iron shoes everywhere; and their pulverized manure, which forms so great a part of the city's dust, and is constantly taken into people's stomachs and lungs, seems to blow more freely about on the asphalt than on the old-fashioned pavements; scraps of paper, straw, fruit-peel, and all manner of minor waste and rubbish, litter both. Every city of the plutocratic world must be an outrage to Altrurian senses, as you already understand, but I doubt if I could ever make you understand the abominable condition of the New York streets during the snowy months of the past winter, when for weeks no attempt was made to remove their accumulated filth. At their best, they would be intolerable to us; at their worst, they are inconceivable and wholly indescribable. The senses witness their condition, but the mind refuses to receive the evidence of the senses; and nothing can be more pathetic, more comic, than the resolution of the New Yorkers in ignoring it.

But if I were once to go into detail, in my effort to make New York intelligible to you, there would be no end to it, and I think I had better get back to my topographical generalities. I have given you some notion of my position at the gate of Central Park, and you must imagine all my studies of the city beginning and ending here. I love to linger near it, because it affords a hope for New York that I feel so distinctly nowhere else in New York, though certain traits of the city's essentially transitional and experimental nature sometimes also suggest that it may be the first city of America to Altrurianize. The upper classes are at least used to the political sway of the lower classes, and when they realize that they never can have any hope but in bettering the lot of their rulers, the end will not be far off, for it will then be seen that this can be lastingly done only through a change of the economic conditions.

In the meantime, the Park, which is the physical heart of New York, is Altrurian already. In the contrasts of rich and poor, which you can no more escape there than you can in the city streets, you are, indeed, afflicted with that sense of absurdity, of impossibility, so comforting to the American when he strives to imagine Altrurian conditions, and gets no farther than to imagine the creatures of a plutocratic civilization in them. He imagines that, in an Altrurian state, people must have the same motives, interests, anxieties, which he has always known them to have, and which they carry with them into Central Park, and only lay aside for a moment in response to the higher appeal which its equal opportunities make. But then, at moments these care-worn, greed-worn souls do put off the burden of their inequality, their superiority or their inferiority, and meet on the same broad level of humanity; and I wish, my dear Cyril, that you would always keep its one great oasis in your thoughts, as you follow me in my wanderings through this vast commercial desert. It is the token, if not the pledge, of happier things, and, while I remain here, it will be always to me a precious image of home.

When I leave it I usually take one of the avenues southward, and then turn eastward or westward on one of the cross-streets whose perspective appeals to my curiosity, and stroll through it to one of the rivers. The avenues, as you will see, are fifteen or sixteen in number, and they stretch, some farther than others, up and down the island, but most of them end in the old town, where its irregularity begins, at the south, and several are inter-

"THEY ALWAYS SUGGEST MONEY, MORE THAN TASTE."

rupted by the different parks at the north. Together with the streets that intersect them between the old town and Central Park, they form one of the most characteristic parts of modern New York. Like the streets, they are numbered, as you know, rather than named, from a want of imagination, or from a preference of mere convenience to the poetry and associations that cluster about a name, and can never cling to a number, or from a business impatience to be quickly done with the matter. This must rather defeat itself, however, when a hurried man undertakes to tell you that he lives at three hundred and seventy-five on One Hundred and Fifty-seventh street. Towards the rivers the avenues grow shabbier and shabbier, though this statement must be qualified, like all general statements. Seventh avenue, on the west, is pleasanter than Sixth avenue, and Second avenue, on the east, is more agreeable than Third avenue. In fact, the other afternoon, as I strayed over to the East river, I found several blocks of Avenue A, which runs nearest it, very quiet, built up with comfortable dwellings, and even clean, as cleanliness is understood in New York.

But it is Fifth avenue which divides the city lengthwise nearest the middle, and it is this avenue which affords the norm of style and comfort to the other avenues on either hand, and to all the streets that intersect it. Madison avenue is its rival, and has suffered less from the invasion of shops and hotels, but a long stretch of Fifth avenue is still the most aristocratic quarter of the city, and is upon the whole its finest thoroughfare. I need not say that we should not, in Altruria, think any New York street fine; but, generally, Fifth avenue and the cross-streets in its better part have a certain regularity in their mansions of brownstone, which recalls to one, if it does not actually give again, the pleasure we get from the symmetry at home. They are at least not so chaotic as they might be, and though they always suggest money more than taste, I cannot at certain moments, and under the favor of an evening sky, deny them a sort of unlovely and forbidding beauty.

There are not many of these cross-streets which have remained intact from the business of the other avenues. They have always a drinking saloon, or a provision store, or an apothecary's shop, at the corners where they intersect; the modistes find lodgment in them almost before the residents are aware. Beyond Sixth avenue, or Seventh at furthest, on the west, and Fourth avenue or Lexington, on the east, they lose their genteel character; their dwellings degenerate into apartment-houses, and then into tenement-houses of lower and lower grade till the rude traffic and the offensive industries of the river shores are reached.

A TYPICAL UP-TOWN CROSS-STREET.

But once more I must hedge, for sometimes a street is respectable almost to the water on one side or the other ; and there are whole neighborhoods of pleasant dwellings far down town, which seem to have been forgotten by the enterprise of business, or neglected by its caprice, and to have escaped for a time at least the contagion of poverty. Business and poverty are everywhere slowly or swiftly eating their way into the haunts of respectability, and destroying its pleasant homes. They already have the whole of the old town to themselves. In large spaces of it no one dwells but the janitors with their families, who keep the sky-scraping edifices where business frets the time away ; and by night, in the streets where myriads throng by day, no one walks but the outcast and the watch.

Many of these business streets are the handsomest in the city, with a good sky line, and an architectural ideal too good for the sordid uses of commerce. This is often realized in antipathetic iron, but often there is good honest work in stone, and an effect better than the best of Fifth avenue. But this is stupid and wasteful, as everything necessarily is in the plutocratic conditions. It is for the pleasure of no one's taste or sense ; the business men who traffic in these edifices have no time for their beauty, or no perception of it; the porters and truckmen and expressmen, who toil and moil in these thoroughfares, have no use for the grandeur that catches the eye of a chance passer from Altruria.

Other spaces are abandoned to the poverty which festers in the squalid houses and swarms day and night in the squalid streets ; but business presses closer and harder upon these refuges of its foster-child, not to say its offspring, and it is only a question of time before it shall wholly possess them. It is only a question of time before all the comfortable quarters of the city, northward from the old town to the Park, shall be invaded, and the people driven to the streets building up on the west and east of it for a little longer sojourn. Where their last stay shall be, heaven knows ; perhaps they will be forced into the country ; or before that happens they may be rescued from themselves by the advance of Altrurianization.

In this sort of invasion, however, it is poverty that seems mostly to come first, and it is business that follows and holds

ARCHITECTURE IN THE WHOLESALE DISTRICT.

the conquest, though this is far from being always the case. Whether it is so or not, however, poverty is certain at some time to impart its taint ; for it is perpetual here, from generation to generation, like death itself. In the plutocratic conditions, poverty is incurable ; the very hope of cure is laughed to scorn by those who cling the closest to these conditions ; it may be better at one time, and worse at another; but it must always be, somehow, till time shall be no more. It is from everlasting to everlasting, they say, with an unconscious blasphemy of the ever-enduring Good, and, unless the conditions change, I must confess that they have reason for their faith in evil.

When I come home from these walks of mine, heart-sick, as I usually do, I have a vision of the wretched quarters through which I have passed, as blotches of disease upon the civic body, as loathsome sores, destined to eat deeper and deeper into it; and I am haunted by this sense of them, until I plunge deep into the Park, and wash my consciousness clean of it all for a while. But when I am actually in these leprous spots, I become hardened, for the moment, to the deeply underlying fact of human discomfort. I feel their picturesqueness, with a devilish indifference to that ruin, or that defect, which must so largely constitute the charm of the picturesque. A street of tenement-houses is always more picturesque than a street of brownstone residences, which the same thoroughfare usually is before it slopes to either river. The fronts of the edifices are decorated with the iron balconies and ladders of the fire-escapes, and have in the perspective a false air of gayety, which is travestied in their rear by the lines thickly woven from the windows to the tall poles set between the backs of the houses, and fluttering with drying clothes as with banners.

The sidewalks swarm with children, and the air rings with their clamor, as they fly back and forth at play; on the thresholds, the mothers sit nursing their babes, and the old women gossip together; young girls lean from the casements, alow and aloft, or flirt from the doorways with the hucksters who leave their carts in the street, while they come forward with some bargain in fruit or vegetables, and then resume their leisurely progress and their jarring cries. The place has all the attraction of close neighborhood, which the poor love, and which affords them for nothing the spectacle of the human drama, with themselves for actors. In a picture it would be most pleasingly effective, for then you could be in it, and yet have the distance on it which it needs. But to be in it, and not have the distance, is to inhale the stenches of the neglected street, and to catch that yet fouler and dreadfuller poverty-smell which breathes from the open doorways. It is to see the children quarrelling in their games, and beating each other in the face, and rolling each other in the gutter, like the little savage outlaws they are. It is to see the work-worn look of the mothers, the squalor of the babes, the haggish ugliness of the old women, the slovenly frowziness of the young girls. All this

"ALL THIS MAKES YOU HASTEN YOUR PACE—"

"SKY-SCRAPING EDIFICES WHERE BUSINESS FRETS THE TIME AWAY."

able self-assertion of business, which is first in the people's thoughts, and must necessarily be given the first place in their cities. Huge factories and foundries, lumber yards, breweries, slaughter-houses and warehouses, abruptly interspersed with stables and hovels, and drinking saloons, disfigure the shore, and in the nearest avenue, the freight trains come and go on lines of railroads, in all this middle portion of New York. South of it, in the business section, the poverty section, the river region is a mere chaos of industrial and commercial strife and pauper wretchedness. North of it there are gardened driveways following the shore ; and even at many points between, when you finally reach the river, there is a kind of peace, or at least a truce to the frantic activities of business. To be sure, the heavy trucks grind up and down the long piers, but on either side the docks are full of leisurely canal-boats, and if you could come with me in the late afternoon, you would see the smoke curling upward from their cabin makes you hasten your pace down to the river, where the tall buildings break and dwindle into stables and shanties of wood, and finally end in the piers, commanding the whole stretch of the mighty waterway with its shipping, and the wooded heights of its western bank.

I am supposing you to have walked down a street of tenement-houses to the North river, as the New Yorkers call the Hudson ; and I wish I could give you some notion of the beauty and majesty of the stream. You must turn to the photographs I send you for that beauty and majesty, and for some sense of the mean and ignoble effect of the city's invasion of the hither shore. The ugliness is, indeed, only worse in degree, but not in kind, than that of all city water-fronts in plutocratic countries. Instead of pleasant homes, with green lawns and orchards sloping to the brink, as we have them in Altruria, they have here the inexor-

"FLUTTERING WITH DRYING CLOTHES AS WITH BANNERS."

"THE MIGHTY WATER-WAY WITH ITS SHIPPING."

roofs, as from the chimneys of so many rustic cottages, and smell the evening meal cooking within, while the canal-wives lounged at the gangway hatches for a breath of the sunset air, and the boatmen smoked on the gunwales or indolently plied the long sweeps of their pumps. All the hurry and turmoil of the city is lost among these people, whose clumsy craft recall the grassy inland levels remote from the metropolis, and the slow movement of life in the quiet country ways. Some of the mothers from the tenement-houses stroll down on the piers with their babies in their arms, and watch their men-kind, of all ages, fishing along the sides of the dock, or casting their lines far out into the current at the end. They do not seem to catch many fish, and never large ones, but they silently enjoy the sport, which they probably find leisure for in the general want of work in these hard times; if they swear a little at their luck, now and then, it is, perhaps, no more than their luck deserves. Some do not even fish, but sit with their legs dangling over the water, and watch the swift tugs, or the lagging sloops that pass, with now and then a larger sail, or a towering passenger steamboat. Far down the stream they can see the forests of masts, fringing either shore, and following the point of the island and round and up into the great channel called the East river. These ships seemed as multitudinous as the houses that spread everywhere from them over the shore further than the eye can reach. They bring the commerce of the world to this mighty city, which, with all its riches, is the parent of such misery, and with all its traffic abounds in idle men who cannot find work. The ships look happy and free, in the stream, but they are of the plutocratic world, too, as well the houses; and let them spread their wings ever so widely, they still bear with them the slavery of the poor, as we know too well from the sorrowful tales of the castaways on our coast.

You must lose the thought of what is below the surface everywhere and in everything in America, if you would possess your soul from the pain perpetually threatening it; and I am afraid, my dear

Cyril, that if you could be suddenly transported to my side, and behold what underlies all life here, with your fresh Altrurian eyes, you would not be more shocked at the sight than at me, who, knowing it all, can ever have a moment's peace in my knowledge. But I do have many moments' peace, through the mere exhaustion of consciousness, and I must own with whatever shame you would have me feel, that sometimes I have moments of pleasure. The other evening I walked over to the East river through one of those tenement streets, and I reached the waterside just as the soft night was beginning to fall in all its autumnal beauty. The afterglow died from the river, while I hung upon a parapet over a gulf ravened out of the bank for a street, and experienced that artistic delight which cultivated people are often proud of feeling here, in the aspect of the long prison island which breaks the expanse of the channel. I knew the buildings on it were prisons, and that the men and women in them, bad before, could only come out of them worse than before, and doomed to a life of outlawry and of crime. I was aware that they were each an image of that loveless and hopeless perdition which the cruelty of men imagines God has prepared for the souls of the damned, but I could not see the barred windows of those hells in the waning light. I could only see the trees along their walks; their dim lawns and gardens, and the castellated forms of the prisons; and the esthetic sense, which in these unhappy lands is careful to keep itself pure from pity, was tickled with an agreeable impression of something old and fair. The dusk thickened, and the vast steamboats which ply between the city and the New England ports on Long Island Sound, and daily convey whole populations of passengers between New York and Boston, began to sweep by silently, swiftly, luminous masses on the black water. Their lights aloft at bow and stern, floated with them like lambent planets; the lights of lesser craft dipped by, and came and went in the distance; the lamps of the nearer and farther shores twinkled into sight, and a peace that ignored all the sorrow of it, fell upon the scene.

It was such peace as can alone come to you in a life like this. If you would have any rest you must ignore a thousand

CANAL BOATS ON THE HUDSON.

"THE WOODED HEIGHTS OF ITS WESTERN BANK."

facts, which, if you recognize them, turn and rend you, and instil their poison into your lacerated soul. In your pleasures you must forget the deprivation which your indulgence implies; if you feast, you must shut out the thought of them that famish; when you lie down in your bed, you cannot sleep if you remember the houseless who have nowhere to lay their heads. You are everywhere beleaguered by the armies of want and woe, and in the still watches of the night you can hear their invisible sentinels calling to one another, "All is ill! All is ill!" and hushing their hosts to the apathy of despair.

Yes, if you would have any comfort of your life here, you must have it in disregard of your fellowmen, your kindred, your brothers, made like yourself and fashioned to the same enjoyments and sufferings, whose hard lot forbids them comfort. This is a fact, however, which the civilization of all plutocratic countries is resolute to deny, and the fortunate children of that civilization try to live in a fiction of the demerit of the unfortunate: they feign that these are more indolent or vicious than themselves, and so are, somehow, condemned by the judgments of God to their abasement and destitution. But at the bottom of their hearts they know that this pretense is false, and that it is a mere chance they are not themselves of the unfortunate. They must shut their minds to this knowledge as they must shut them to the thought of all the misery which their prosperity is based on, or, as I say, they can have no peace.

You can reason to the effect upon character among them, among the best of them. It is a consequence which you would find unspeakably shocking, yet which, if you personally knew their conditions, you would be lenient to, for you would perceive that, while the conditions endure, there is no help, no hope for them. The wonder is that, in such circumstances as theirs, they ever permit their sympathies the range that these sometimes

"THE CASTELLATED FORMS OF THE PRISONS."

take, only to return upon them in an anguish of impotency. None but the shortsighted and thoughtless in a plutocracy can lastingly satisfy themselves even with a constant giving, for the thoughtful know that charity corrupts and debases, and that finally it is no remedy. So these take refuge from themselves in a wilful ignorance, sometimes lasting, sometimes transient, of the things in their life that disturb and displease them. It is the only thing to do here, my dear Cyril, and I will not deny that I have come to do it, like the rest. Since I cannot relieve the wrong I see, I have learned often to shut my eyes to it, with the effect, which most Americans experience, that, since there seems to be no way of righting the wrong, the wrong must be a sort of right. Yes, this infernal juggle of the mind operates itself in me, too, at times, so that I doubt the reality of my whole happy life in the past, I doubt Altruria, I doubt you.

I beseech you, therefore, to write me as often as you can, and as fully and vividly. Tell me of our country, remind me of the state where men dwell together as brothers; use every device to make it living and real to me; for here I often lose the memory and the sense of it, and at all times I have a weakened sense of the justice and mercy that I once thought ruled this world, but which the Americans think rules only the world to come.

A. HOMOS.

"THE VAST STEAMBOATS SWEEP SILENTLY BY."

LETTERS OF AN ALTRURIAN TRAVELLER.

BY W. D. HOWELLS.

PLUTOCRATIC CONTRASTS AND CONTRADICTIONS.

V.

New York, November 15, 1893.

My dear Cyril:

In my last I tried to give you some notion of the form and structure of this strange city, but I am afraid that I did it very vaguely and insufficiently. I do not suppose that I could ever do it fully, and perhaps the attempt was foolish. But I hope that I may, without greater folly, at least offer to share with you the feeling I have concerning American life, and most of all concerning New York life, that it is forever on the way, and never arrives. This is the effect that I constantly receive in the streets here and especially in the avenues, which are fitly named so far as avenue means approach merely. They are roadways which people get back and forth by, in their haste from nowhere to nowhere, as it would seem to us. Of course they do physically reach their places of business downtown in the morning, and their places of eating and sleeping uptown in the evening; but morally they are forever in transition. Whether they are bent upon business, or bent upon pleasure, the Americans, or certainly the New Yorkers, perpetually postpone the good of life, as we know it in Altruria, and as it is known in some tranquiller countries even of the plutocratic world. They make money, but they do not have money, for there is no such thing as the sensible possession of money, and hardly of the things that money can buy. They seek enjoyment and they find excitement, for joy is the blessing of God, and like every good gift comes unsought, and flies pursuit. They know this, as well as we do, and in certain moments of dejection, in the hours of pain, in the days of sorrow, they realize it, but at other times they ignore it. If they did not ignore it they could not live, they say, and they appear to think that by ignoring it they do live, though to me there is nothing truly vital in their existence.

The greatest problem of their metropolis

is not how best to be in this place or that, but how fastest to go from one to the other, and they have made guesses at the riddle, bad and worse, on each of the avenues, which, in their character of mere roadways, look as if the different car-tracks had been in them first, and the buildings, high and low, had chanced along their sides afterwards. This is not the fact, of course, and it is not so much the effect on Fifth avenue, and Madison avenue, and Lexington avenue, which are streets of dwellings, solidly built up, like the cross streets. But it is undoubtedly the effect on all the other avenues, in great part of their extent. They vary but little in appearance otherwise, from east to west, except so far as the elevated railroads disfigure them, if thoroughfares so shabby and repulsive as they mostly are, can be said to be disfigured, and not beautified by whatever can be done to hide any part of their ugliness. Where this is left to make its full impression upon the spectator, there are lines of horse-cars perpetually jingling up and down except on Fifth avenue, where they have stages, as the New Yorkers call the unwieldly and unsightly vehicles that ply there, and on Second avenue, where they have electric cars, something like our own, in principle. But the horse-cars run even under the elevated tracks, and you have absolutely no experience of noise in the Altrurian life which can enable you to conceive of the hellish din that bursts upon the sense when at some corner two cars encounter on the parallel tracks below, while two trains roar and shriek and hiss on the rails overhead, and a turmoil of rattling express wagons, heavy drays and trucks, and carts, hacks, carriages and huge vans rolls itself between and beneath the prime agents of the uproar. The noise is not only deafening, it is bewildering: you cannot know which side the danger threatens most, and you literally take your life in your hand when you cross in the midst of it. Broadway, which traverses the district I am thinking of, in a diagonal line till it loses its distinctive character beyond the Park, is the course of the cable cars. These are propelled by an endless chain running underneath the pavement with a silent speed that is more dangerous even than the tumultuous rush on the avenues. Now and then the apparatus for gripping the chain will not release it, and then the car rushes wildly over the track, running amuck through everything in its way, and spreading terror on every hand. When under control the long saloons advance swiftly, from either direction, at intervals of half a minute, with a monotonous alarum of their gongs, and the foot passenger has to look well to his way if he ventures

"YOU TAKE YOUR LIFE IN YOUR HAND WHEN YOU CROSS IN THE MIDST OF IT."

across the track, lest in avoiding one car another roll him under its wheels.

Apparently, the danger is guarded as well as it can be, and it has simply to be taken into the account of life in New York, for it cannot be abated, and no one is to be blamed for what is the fault of everyone. It is true that there ought not, perhaps, to be any track in such a thoroughfare, but it would be hard to prove that people could get on without it, as they did before the theft of the street for the original horse-car track. Perhaps it was not a theft; but at all events, and at the best, the street was given away by the city to an adventurer who wished to lay the tracks in it for his private gain, and none of the property owners along the line could help themselves. There is nothing that the Americans hold so dear, you know, or count so sacred, as private property; life and limb are cheap in comparison; but private enterprise is allowed to violate the rights of private property, from time to time here, in the most dramatic way.

I do not speak, now, of the railroad companies, which have gridironed the country, in its whole length and breadth, and which are empowered by their franchises to destroy the homes of the living and desecrate the graves of the dead, in running their lines from point to point. These companies do pay something, as little as they may, or as much as they must; but the street-car company which took possession of Broadway never paid the abuttors anything, I believe; and the elevated railroad companies are still resisting payment of damages on the four avenues which they occupied for their way up and down the city without offering compensation to the property owners along their route. If the community had built these roads, it would have indemnified everyone, for the community is always just when it is the expression of the common honesty here; and if it is ever unjust, it is because the uncommon dishonesty has contrived to corrupt it.

Yet the Americans trust themselves so little in their civic embodiment that the movement for the public ownership of the railroads makes head slowly against an inconceivable prejudice. Last winter, when the problem of rapid transit pressed sorely upon the New Yorkers, the commission in charge could find no way to solve it but by offering an extension of franchise to the corporation which has already the monopoly of it. There was no question of the city's building the roads, and working them at cost; and if there had been, there would have been no question of submitting the project to those whose interests are involved. They have no such thing here as the referendum, and the Americans who are supposed to make their own laws, merely elect their representatives, and have no voice themselves in approving or condemning legislation.

The elevated roads and the cable road had no right to be, on the terms that the New Yorkers have them, but they are by far the best means of transit in the city, and I must say that if they were not abuses, they would offer great comfort and great facility to the public. This is especially true of the elevated roads, which, when you can put their moral offense out of your mind, are always delightful in their ease and airy swiftness. The tracks are lifted upon iron piers, from twenty to fifty feet above the street, according to the inequality of the surface, and you fly smoothly along between the second and third story windows of the houses, which are shops below and dwellings above, on the avenues. The stations, though they have the prevailing effect of over-use, and look dirty and unkempt, are rather pretty in themselves; and you reach them, at frequent intervals, by flights of not ungraceful iron steps. The elevated roads are always picturesque, with here and there a sweeping curve that might almost be called beautiful.

They darken the avenues, of course, and fill them with an abominable uproar. Yet traffic goes underneath, and life goes

"THE INTERMINABLE TUNNELS."

on alongside and overhead, and the city has adjusted itself to them, as a man adjusts himself to a chronic disease. I do not know whether they add to the foulness of the streets they pass through or not; I hardly think they do. The mud lies longer, after a rain, in the interminable tunnels which they form over the horse-car tracks in the middle of the avenues, and which you can look through for miles; but the mud does not blow into your nose and mouth as the dust does, and that is, so far, a positive advantage. A negative advantage, which I have hinted, is that they hide so much of the street from sight, and keep you from seeing all its foulness and shabbiness, pitilessly open to the eye in the avenues which have only horse-car tracks in them. In fact, now that the elevated railroads are built, and the wrong they have done to persons is mainly past recall, perhaps the worst that can be said of them is that they do not serve their purpose. Of course, in plutocratic conditions, where ten men are always doing the work of one man in rivalry with each other, the passage of people to and from business is enormous:

to get money, and the passage of women to spend it; and at the hours of the morning and the afternoon when the volume of travel is the greatest, the trains of the elevated roads offer a spectacle that is really incredible.

Every seat in them is taken, and every foot of space in the aisle between the seats is held by people standing, and swaying miserably to and fro by the leather straps dangling from the roofs. Men and women are indecently crushed together, without regard for that personal dignity which we prize, but which the Americans seem to know nothing of and care nothing for. The multitude overflows from the car, at either end, and the passengers are as tightly wedged on the platforms without as they are within. The long trains follow each other at intervals of two or three minutes, and at each station they make a stop of but a few seconds, when those who wish to alight fight their way through the struggling mass. Those who wish to mount fight their way into the car or onto the platform, where the guard slams an iron gate against the stomachs and in the faces of those arriving too late. Sometimes horrible accidents happen; a man clinging to the outside of the gate has the life crushed out of his body against the posts of the station as the train pulls out. But in this land, where people have such a dread of civic collectivism of any kind, lest individuality should suffer, the individual is practically nothing in the regard of the corporate collectivities which abound.

It is not only the corporations which outrage personal rights, in America; where there is a question of interest, there seems to be no question of rights between individuals. They prey upon one another and seize advantages by force and by fraud in too many ways for me to hope to make the whole situation evident to you, but I may at least give you some notion of the wrong they do. The avenues to the eastward and westward have not grown up solidly and continuously in obedience to any law of order, or in pursuance of any meditated design. They have been pushed along given lines, in fragments, as builders saw their interest in offering buyers a house or a row of houses, or as they could glut or trick the greed of land-owners clinging to their land, and counting upon some need of it, in the hope of extorting an unearned profit from it. In one place you will see a vast and lofty edifice, of brick or stone, and on each side of it or in front of it, a structure one-fourth as high, or a row of scurvy hovels, left there till a purchaser comes, not to pay the honest worth of the land for it, but to yield the price the owner wants. In other places you see long stretches of high board fence, shutting in vacant lots, usually the best lots on the street, which the landlord holds for the rise destined to accrue to him from the building all round and beyond his property. In the meantime he pays a low tax on his land compared with the tax which the improved property pays, and gets some meager return for the use of his fence by the Italian fruiterers who build their stalls into it, and by the bill-posters who cover it with a medley of theatrical announcements, picturing the scenes of the different plays and the persons of the players. To the Altrurian public the selfishness of a man willing idly to benefit by the industry and energy of others in giving value to his possessions would be unimaginable. Yet this is so common here that it is accepted and honored as a proof of business sagacity; and the man who knows how to hold onto his land, until the very moment when it can enrich him most, though he has neither plowed nor sown it, or laid the foundation of a human dwelling upon it, is honored as a longheaded and solid citizen, who deserves well of his neighbors. There are many things which unite

"THE STATIONS ARE RATHER PRETTY IN THEMSELVES."

"A PRECIPITOUS FALL OF TWELVE STORIES."

to render the avenues unseemly and unsightly, such as the apparently desperate tastelessness and the apparently instinctive uncleanliness of the New Yorkers. But as I stand at some point commanding a long stretch of one of their tiresome perspectives, which is architecturally like nothing so much as a horse's jawbone, with the teeth broken or dislodged at intervals, I can blame nothing so much for the hideous effect as the rapacity of the land-owner holding on for a rise, as it is called. It is he who breaks the sky-line, and keeps the street, mean and poor at the best in design, a defeated purpose, and a chaos come again.

Even when the owners begin to build, to improve their real estate, as the phrase is, it is without regard to the rights of their neighbors, or the feelings or tastes of the public, so far as the public may be supposed to have any. This is not true of the shabbier avenues alone, but of the finest, and of all the streets. If you will look, for instance, at the enclosed photograph of the street facing the southern limit of the Park, you will get some notion of what I mean, and I hope you will be willing to suffer by a little study of it. At the western end you will see a vacant lot, with its high board fence covered with painted signs, then a tall mass of apartment houses ; then a stretch of ordinary New York dwellings of the old commonplace brownstone sort ; then a stable, and a wooden liquor saloon at the corner. Across the next avenue there rises far aloof the compact bulk of a series of apartment houses, which in color and design are the pleasantest in the city, and are so far worthy of their site. Beyond them to the eastward the buildings decline and fall, till they sink into another wooden drinking-shop on the corner of another avenue, where you will see the terminus of one of the elevated roads. Beyond this avenue is the fence of a large vacant lot, covered, as usual, with theatrical posters, and then there surges skyward another series of apartment houses. The highest of these is nearly fifty feet higher than its nearest neighbors, which sink again, till you suddenly drop from their nondescript monotony to the gothic façade of a house of a wholly different color, in its pale sandstone, from the red of their brick fronts.

A vacant lot yawns here again, with a flare of theatrical posters on its fence, and beyond this, on the corner, is a huge hotel, the most agreeable of the three that tower above the fine square at the gate of the Park. With that silly American weakness for something foreign, this square is called the Plaza ; I believe that it is not at all like a Spanish plaza, but the name is its least offense. An irregular space in the center is planted with trees, in whose shade the broken-kneed hacks of the public carriages droop their unhappy heads, without the spirit to bite the flies that trouble their dreams; and below this you get a glimpse of the conventional cross-street terminating the Plaza. At the eastern corner of the avenue is a vacant lot, with pictorial advertisements painted on its fence, and then you come to the second of the great hotels which give the Plaza such character as it has. It is of a light-colored stone, and it towers far above the first, which is of brick. It is thirteen stories high, and it stops abruptly in a flat roof. On the next corner north is another hotel, which rises six or seven stories higher yet, and terminates in a sort of mansard, topping a romanesque cliff of yellow brick and red sandstone. I seek a term for the architectural order, but it may not be the right one. There is no term for the civic disorder of what succeeds. From the summit of this enormous acclivity there is a precipitous fall of twelve stories to the roof of the next edifice, which is a

"THERE ARE CERTAIN BITS OF QUAINTNESS."

grocery; and then to the florist's and photographer's next is another descent of three stories; on the corner is a drinking-saloon, one story in height, with a brick front and a wooden side. I will not ask you to go farther with me; the avenue continues northward and southward in a delirium of lines and colors, a savage anarchy of shapes, which I should think the general experience of the beauty of the Fair City at Chicago would now render perceptible even to the dull American sense. What exists is the necessary and inexorable effect of that uncivic individuality which the Americans prize, and which can manifest itself only in harm and wrong; but if you criticised it you would surprise and alarm them almost as much as if you attacked the atrocious economic inequality it springs from.

There are other points on Fifth avenue nearly as bad as this, but not quite, and there are long stretches of it, which, if dull, have at least a handsome uniformity. I have told you already that it is still upon the whole, the best of the avenues, in the sense of being the abode of the best, that is the richest people; the Americans habitually use best in this sense. Madison avenue stretches northwest farther than the eye can reach, an interminable perspective of brownstone dwellings, as yet little invaded by business. Lexington avenue is of the same character, but of a humbler sort. On Second avenue, down town, there are large old mansions of the time when Fifth avenue was still the home of the parvenus; and at different points on such other avenues as are spared by the elevated roads, there are blocks of decent and comfortable dwellings; but for the most part they are wholly given up to shops. Of course, these reiterate with the insane wastefulness of the competitive system the same business, the same enterprise, a thousand times. The Americans have no conception of our distribution; and though nearly everything they now use is made in large establishments, their wares are dispersed and sold in an infinitude of small stores.

One hears a good deal about the vast emporiums which are gathering the retail trade into themselves, and devastating the minor commerce, but there are perhaps a score of these at most, in New York; and on the shabbier avenues and cross-streets there are at least a hundred miles of little shops, where an immense population of little dealers levy tribute on the public through the profit they live by. Until you actually see this, you can hardly conceive of such a multitude of people taken away from the labor due to all from all, and solely devoted to marketing the things made by people who are overworked in making them. But bad as this is, and immoral as it is in Altrurian eyes, it is really harmless beside a traffic which is the most conspicuous on these avenues; I mean the traffic in intoxicating liquors, sold and drunk on the premises. I need not tell you that I still hold our national principles concerning the use of alcohol, but I have learned here to be lenient to its use, in a measure which you would not perhaps excuse. I perceive that as long as there is poverty there must be drunkenness, until the State interferes and sells a man only so much as he can safely drink. Yet, knowing as I do from the daily witness of the press and the courts, that drink is the source of most of the crimes and vices which curse this people, I find the private traffic in alcohol infinitely shocking, and the spectacle of it incredible. There is scarcely a block on any of the poorer avenues which has not its liquor store, and generally there are two; wherever a street crosses them there is a saloon on at least one of the corners; sometimes on two, sometimes on three, sometimes even on all four. I had one day the curiosity to count the saloons on Sixth avenue, between the Park, and the point down town where the avenue properly ends. In a stretch of some two miles I counted ninety of them, besides the eating houses where you can buy drink with your meat; and this avenue is probably far less infested with the traffic than some others.

You may therefore safely suppose that out of the hundred miles of shops, there are ten, or fifteen, or twenty miles of saloons. They have the best places on the avenues, and on the whole they make the handsomest show. They all have a cheerful and inviting look, and if you step within, you find them cosy, quiet, and for New York, clean. There are commonly tables set about in them, where their frequenters can take their beer or whisky at their ease, and eat the free lunch which is often given in them; in a rear room you see a billiard table. In fact, they form the poor man's clubhouses and if he might resort to them with his family, and be in the control of the State as to the amount he should spend and drink there, I could not think them without their rightful place in an economy which saps the vital forces of the laborer with overwork, or keeps him in a fever of hope or a fever of despair, as to the chances of getting or not getting work when he has lost it. We at home, have so long passed the sad necessity to which such places minister, that we sometimes forget it, but you know how in our old competitive days, this traffic was one of the first to be taken out of private hands, and assumed by the State, which continued to manage it without a profit so long as the twin crazes of competition and drunkenness endured among us. If you suggested this to the average American, however, he would be horror-struck. He would tell you that what you proposed was little better than anarchy; that in a free country you must always leave private persons free to debauch men's souls and bodies with drink, and make money out of their ruin; that anything else was contrary to human nature, and an invasion of the sacred rights of the individual. Here in New York, this valuable principle is so scrupulously respected, that the saloon controls the municipality, and the New Yorkers think this is much better than for the municipality to control the saloon. It is from the saloon that their political bosses rise to power; it is in the saloon that all the election frauds are planned and fostered; and it

"LONG STRETCHES OF HIGH BOARD FENCE USED BY THE BILL-POSTERS."

would be infinitely comic, if it were not so pathetic, to read the solemn homilies on these abuses in the journals which hold by the good old American doctrine of private trade in drink as one of the bulwarks of their constitution, and a chief defense against the advance of Altrurian ideas.

Without it, there would be far less poverty than there is, but poverty is a good old American institution, too; there would inevitably be less inequality, but inequality is as dear to the American heart as liberty itself. In New York the inequality has that effect upon the architecture which I have tried to give you some notion of; but in fact it deforms life here at every turn, and in nothing more than in the

"A ROW OF CARTS DRAWN UP BY THE STREET-SIDE."

dress of the people, high and low. New York is, on the whole, without doubt, the best dressed community in America, or at least there is a certain number of people here, more expensively and scrupulously attired than you will find anywhere else in the country. I do not say beautifully, for their dress is of the fashion which you have seen in our Regionic museum, where we used to laugh over it together when we fancied people in it, and is a modification of the fashions that prevail everywhere in plutocratic Christendom. The rich copy the fashion set for them in Paris or in London, and then the less rich, and the still less rich, down to the poor, follow them as they can, until you arrive at the very poorest, who wear the cast-off and tattered fashions of former years, and masquerade in a burlesque of the fortunate that never fails to shock and grieve me. They must all somehow be clothed; the climate and the custom require it; but sometimes I think their nakedness would be less offensive; and when I meet a wretched man, with his coat out at elbows, or split up the back, in broken shoes, battered hat, and frayed trousers, or some old woman or young girl in a worn-out, second-hand gown and bonnet, tattered and threadbare and foul, I think that if I were an American, as I am an Altrurian, I would uncover my head to them, and ask their forgiveness for the system that condemns some one always to such humiliation as theirs.

The Americans say such people are not humiliated, that they do not mind it, that they are used to it; but if they ever look these people in the eye, and see the shrinking, averted glance of their shame and tortured pride, they must know that what they say is a cruel lie. At any rate, the presence of these outcasts must spoil the beauty of any dress near them, and there is always so much more penury than affluence that the sight of the crowd in the New York streets must give more pain than pleasure. The other day on Fifth avenue, it did not console me to meet a young and lovely girl, exquisitely dressed in the last effect of Paris, after I had just parted from a young fellow who had begged me to give him a little money to get something to eat, for he had been looking for work a week and had got nothing. I suppose I ought to have doubted his word, he was so decently clad, but I had a present vision of him in rags, and I gave to the frowzy tramp he must soon become.

Of course, this social contrast was extreme, like some of those architectural contrasts I have been noting, but it was by no means exceptional, as those were not. In fact, I do not know but I may say that it was characteristic of the place, though you might say that the prevalent American slovenliness was also characteristic of the New York street crowds; I mean the slovenliness of the men; the women, of whatever order they are, are always as much dandies as they can be. But most American men are too busy to look much after their dress, and when they are very well to do they care very little for it. You see few men dressed with the distinction of the better class of Londoners, and when you do meet them, they have the air of playing a part, as in fact they are: they are playing the part of men of leisure in a nation of men whose reality is constant work, whether they work for bread or whether they work for money, and who, when they are at work, outdo the world, but sink, when they are at leisure, into something third rate and fourth rate. The commonness of effect in the street crowds, is not absent from Fifth avenue or from Madison avenue any more than it is from First avenue or Tenth avenue; and the tide of wealth and fashion that rolls up and down the better avenues in the splendid carriages, makes the shabbiness of the foot-passenger, when he is shabby, as he often is, the more apparent. On the far east side, and on the far west side, the horse-cars, which form the only means of transit, have got the dirt and grime of the streets and the dwellings on them and in them, and there is one tone of foulness in the passengers and the vehicles. I do not wish to speak other than tenderly of the poor but it is useless to pretend that they are other than offensive in aspect, and I have to take my sympathy in both hands when I try to bestow it upon them. Neither they nor the quarter they live in has any palliating quaintness; and the soul, starved of beauty, will seek in vain to feed itself with the husks of picturesqueness in their aspect.

As I have said before, the shabby avenues have a picturesqueness of their own, but it is a repulsive picturesqueness, as I have already suggested, except at a distance. There are some differences of level, on the avenues near the rivers, that give them an advantage of the more central avenues, and there is now and then a break of their line by the water, which is always good. I noticed this particularly on the eastern side of the city, which is also the older part, and which has been less subject to the changes perpetually going on elsewhere, so that First avenue has really a finer sky-line, in many parts, than most parts of Fifth avenue. There are certain bits, as the artists say, in the old quarters of the town once forming Greenwich village, which, when I think of them, make me almost wish to take back what I have said of the absence even of quaintness in New York. If I recall the aspect of Mulberry Bend and Elizabeth street, on a mild afternoon, when their Italian denizens are all either on the pavement or have their heads poked out of the windows, I am still more in doubt of my own words. But I am sure, at least, that there is no kindliness in the quaintness, such as you are said to find in European cities. It has undergone the same sort of malign change here that has transformed the Italians from the friendly folk we are told they are at home, to the surly race, and even savage race they mostly show themselves here: shrewd for their advancement in the material things, which seem the only good things to the Americanized aliens of all races, and fierce for their full share of the political pottage. The Italians have a whole region of the city to themselves, and they might feel at home in it if something more than the filth of their native environment could repatriate them.

As you pass through these streets, there is much to appeal to your pity in the squalid aspect of the people and the place, but nothing to take your fancy; and perhaps this is best, for I think that there is nothing more infernal than the juggle that

"MULBERRY BEND."

A BIT OF GREENWICH VILLAGE.

transmutes for the tenderest hearted people here the misery of their fellows into something comic or poetic. Only very rarely have I got any relief from the sheer distress which the prevalent poverty gives; and perhaps you will not be able to understand how I could find this in the sight of some chickens going to roost on a row of carts drawn up by the street side, near a little hovel where some old people lived in a temporary respite from the building about them; or from a cottage in outlying suburban fields, with a tar-roofed shanty for a stable, and an old horse cropping the pasturage of the enclosure, with a brood of turkeys at his heels.

But in New York you come to be glad of anything that will suggest a sweeter and a gentler life than that which you mostly see. The life of the poor here seemed to me symbolized in a waste and ruined field that I came upon the other day in one of the westward avenues, which had imaginably once been the grounds about a pleasant home, or perhaps a public square. Till I saw this I did not think any piece of our mother earth could have been made to look so brutal and desolate amidst the habitations of men. But every spear of grass had been torn from it; the hardened and barren soil was furrowed and corrugated like a haggard face, and it was all strewn with clubs and stones, as if it had been a savage battleground. A few trees, that seemed beaten back, stood aloof from the borders next the streets, where some courses of an ancient stone wall rose in places above the pavement. I found the sight of it actually depraving; it made me feel ruffianly, and I mused upon it in helpless wonder as to the influence its ugliness must have had amidst the structural ugliness all about it, if some wretch had turned it in hopes of respite.

But probably none ever does. Probably the people on the shabby streets and avenues are no more sensible of their hideousness than the people in the finer streets and avenues are aware of their dulness or their frantic disproportion. I have never heard a New Yorker speak of these things, and I have no doubt that if my words could come to the eyes of the average cultivated New Yorker he would be honestly surprised that any one should find his city so ugly as it is. Dirty he would cheerfully allow it to be, and he would be rather proud of telling you how much New York spent every year for not having herself cleaned; but that she was ludicrously and wilfully ugly he could not believe. As for that first lesson of civilization which my words implicate, a civic control of the private architecture of the place, he would shrink from it with about as much horror as from civic control of the liquor trade. If he did not, he would still be unable to understand how the individual liberty that suffers a man to build offensively to his neighbor or to the public at large, is not liberty, but is a barbarous tyranny, which puts an end instantly to beauty, and extinguishes the common and the personal rights of every one who lives near the offender or passes by his edifice. The Americans are yet so far lost in the dark ages as to suppose that there is freedom where the caprice of one citizen can interfere with the comfort or pleasure of the rest.

A. Homos.

ON THE EAST SIDE.

LETTERS OF AN ALTRURIAN TRAVELLER.

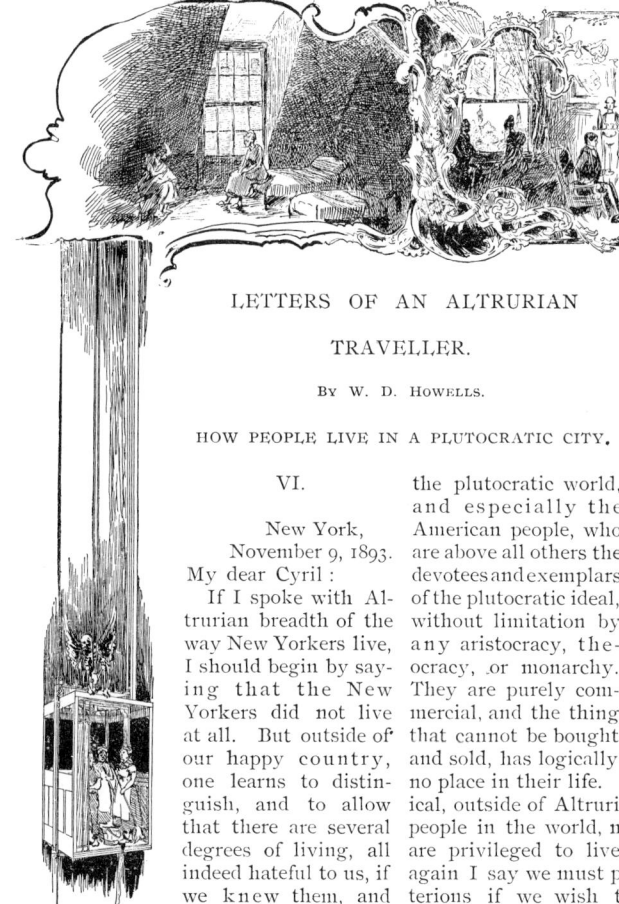

BY W. D. HOWELLS.

HOW PEOPLE LIVE IN A PLUTOCRATIC CITY.

VI.

New York, November 9, 1893.

My dear Cyril:

If I spoke with Altrurian breadth of the way New Yorkers live, I should begin by saying that the New Yorkers did not live at all. But outside of our happy country, one learns to distinguish, and to allow that there are several degrees of living, all indeed hateful to us, if we knew them, and yet none without some saving grace in it. You would say that in conditions where men were embattled against one another by the greed, and the envy, and the ambition which these conditions perpetually appeal to, there could be no grace in life; but we must remember that men have always been better than their conditions, and that otherwise they would have remained savages without the instinct or the wish to advance. Indeed, our own state is testimony of a potential civility in all states, which we must keep in mind when we judge the peoples of the plutocratic world, and especially the American people, who are above all others the devotees and exemplars of the plutocratic ideal, without limitation by any aristocracy, theocracy, or monarchy. They are purely commercial, and the thing that cannot be bought and sold, has logically no place in their life. But life is not logical, outside of Altruria; we are the only people in the world, my dear Cyril, who are privileged to live reasonably; and again I say we must put by our own criterions if we wish to understand the Americans, or to recognize that measure of loveliness which their warped, and stunted, and perverted lives certainly show, in spite of theory and in spite of conscience, even. I can make this clear to you, I think, by a single instance, say that of the American who sees a case of distress, and longs to relieve it. If he is rich, he can give relief with a good conscience, except for the harm that may come to his beneficiary from being helped; but if he is not rich, or not finally rich, and especially if he has a family dependent upon him, he cannot give in anything like the measure Christ bade us give, without wronging those dear to him, immediately or remotely. That is to say, in conditions which oblige every man to look out for himself, a man cannot be a Christian without remorse; he cannot do a generous action without self-reproach; he cannot be nobly unselfish without the fear of being a fool. You would think that this predicament must deprave, and so without doubt it does; and yet it is not wholly depraving. It often has its effect in character of a rare and pathetic sublimity; and many Americans take all the cruel risks of doing good, reckless of the evil that may befall them, and defiant of the upbraidings of their own hearts. This is something that we Altrurians can scarcely understand: it is like the munificence of a savage who has killed a deer and shares it with his starving tribesmen, forgetful of the hungering little ones who wait his return from the chase with food; for life in plutocratic countries is still a chase, and the game is wary and sparse, as the terrible average of failures witnesses.

Of course, I do not mean that Americans may not give at all without sensible risk, or that giving among them is always followed by a logical regret; but as I said, life with them is in nowise logical. They even applaud one another for their charities, which they measure by the amount given, rather than by the love that goes with the giving. The widow's mite has little credit with them, but the rich man's million has an acclaim that reverberates through their newspapers long after his gift is made. It is only the poor in America who do charity as we do by giving help where it is needed; the Americans are mostly too busy, if they are at all prosperous, to give anything but money; and the more money they give, the more charitable they esteem themselves. From time to time some man with twenty or thirty millions gives one of them away, usually to a public institution of some sort, where it will have no effect with the people who are underpaid for their work, or cannot get work; and then his deed is famed throughout the continent as a thing really beyond praise. Yet any one who thinks about it must know that he never earned the millions he kept, or the million he gave, but made them from the labor of others somehow; that with all the wealth left him, he cannot miss the fortune he lavishes any more than if the check which conveyed it were a withered leaf, and not in anywise so much as an ordinary workingman might feel the bestowal of a postage stamp.

But in this study of the plutocratic mind, always so fascinating to me, I am getting altogether away from what I meant to tell you. I meant to tell you not how Americans live in the spirit, however illogically, however blindly and blunderingly, but how they live in the body, and more especially how they house themselves in this city of New York. A great many of them do not house themselves at all, but that is a class which we cannot now consider, and I will speak only of those who have some sort of roof over their heads.

Formerly the New Yorker lived in one of three different ways: in private houses, or boarding-houses, or hotels; there were few restaurants or public tables outside of the hotels, and those who had lodgings, and took their meals at eating-houses were but a small proportion of the whole number. The old classification still holds in a measure, but within the last thirty years, or ever since the Civil War, when the enormous commercial expansion of the country began, several different ways of living have been opened. The first and most noticeable of these is housekeeping in flats, or apartments of three or four rooms or more, on the same floor, as in all the countries of Europe except England; though the flat is now making itself known in London, too. Before the war, the New Yorker who kept house did so in a separate house, three or four stories in height, with a street door of its own. Its pattern within was fixed by long usage, and seldom varied; without, it was of brown-stone before, and brick behind, with an open space there for drying clothes, which was sometimes gardened or planted with trees and vines. The rear of the city blocks which these houses formed was more attractive than the front, as you may still see in the vast succession of monotonous cross-streets not yet invaded by poverty or business; and often the perspective of these areas is picturesque and pleasing. But with the sudden growth of the population when peace came, and through the acquaintance the hordes of

American tourists had made with European fashions of living, it became easy, or at least simple, to divide the floors of many of these private dwellings into apartments, each with its own kitchen and all the apparatus of housekeeping. The apartments then had the street entrance and the stairways in common, and they had in common the cellar and the furnace for heating; they had in common the disadvantage of being badly aired and badly lighted. They were dark, cramped and uncomfortable, but they were cheaper than separate houses, and they were more homelike than boarding-houses or hotels. Large numbers of them still remain in use, and when people began to live in flats, in conformity with the law of evolution, many buildings were put up and subdivided into apartments in imitation of the old dwellings which had been changed into them.

But the apartment as the New Yorkers now mostly have it, was at the same time evolving from another direction. The poorer class of New York work-people had for a long period before the war lived, as they still live, in vast edifices, once thought prodigiously tall, which were called tenement houses. In these a family of five or ten persons is commonly packed in two or three rooms, and even in one room, where they eat and sleep, without the amenities and often without the decencies of life, and of course without light and air. The buildings in case of fire are death-traps; but the law obliges the owners to provide some apparent means of escape, which they do in the form of iron balconies and ladders giving that festive air to their façades which I have already noted. The bare and dirty entries and stair-cases are really ramifications of the filthy streets without, and each tenement opens upon a landing as if it opened upon a public thoroughfare. The rents extorted from the inmates is sometimes a hundred per cent., and is nearly always cruelly out of proportion to the value of the houses, not to speak of the wretched shelter afforded; and when the rent is not paid the family in arrears is set with all its poor household gear upon the sidewalk, in a pitiless indifference to the season and the weather, which you could not realize without seeing it, and which is incredible even of plutocratic nature. Of course, landlordism, which you have read so much of, is at its worst in the case of the tenement houses. But you must understand that comparatively few people in New York own the roofs that shelter them. By far the greater number live, however they live, in houses owned by others, by a class who prosper and grow rich, or richer, simply by owning the roofs over other men's heads. The landlords have, of course, no human relation with their tenants, and really no business relations, for all the affairs between them are transacted by agents. Some have the repute of being better than others; but they all live, or expect to live, without work, on their rents. They are very much respected for it; the rents are considered a just return from the money invested. You must try to conceive of this as an actual fact, and not merely as a statistical statement. I know it will not be easy for you; it is not easy for me, though I have it constantly before my face.

The tenement house, such as it is, is the original of the apartment house, which perpetuates some of its most characteristic features on a scale and in material undreamt of in the simple philosophy of the inventor of the tenement house. The worst of these features is the want of light and air, but as much more space, and as many more rooms are conceded as the tenant will pay for. The apartment house, however, soars to heights that the tenement house never half reached, and is sometimes ten stories high. It is built fire-proof, very often, and it is generally equipped with an elevator, which runs night and day, and makes one level of all the floors. The cheaper sort, or those which have departed less from the tenement house original, have no elevators, but the street door in all is kept shut and locked, and is opened only by the tenant's latchkey, or by the janitor having charge of the whole building. In the finer houses, there is a page whose sole duty it is to open and shut this door, and who is usually brass buttoned to one blinding effect of livery with the elevator boy. Where this page or hall-boy is found, the elevator carries you to the door of any apartment you seek; where he is not found, there is a bell and a speaking-tube in the lower entry, for each apartment, and you ring up the occupant, and talk to him as many stories off as he happens to be. But people who can afford to indulge their pride will not live in this sort of apartment house, and the rents in them are much lower than in the finer sort. The finer sort are vulgarly fine for the most part, with a gaudy splendor of mosaic pavement, marble stairs, frescoed ceilings, painted walls, and cabinet woodwork. But there are many that are fine in a good taste, in the things that are common to the inmates. Their fittings for housekeeping are of all degrees of perfection, and except for the want of light and air, life in them has a high degree of gross luxury. They are heated throughout with pipes of steam or hot water, and they are sometimes lighted with both gas and electricity, which the inmate uses at will, though of course at his own cost. Outside, they are the despair of architecture, for no style has yet been invented which enables the artist to characterize them with beauty, and wherever they lift their vast bulks they deform the whole neighborhood, throwing the other buildings out of scale, and making it impossible for future edifices to assimilate themselves to the intruder.

There is no end to these apartment houses for multitude, and there is no street or avenue free from them. Of course the better sort are to be found on the fashionable avenues and the finer cross-streets, but others follow the course of the horse-car lines on the eastern and western avenues, and the elevated roads on the avenues which these have invaded. In such places they are shops below and apartments above, and I cannot see that the inmates seem at all sensible that they are unfitly housed in them. People are born and married, and live and die in the midst of an uproar so frantic that you would think they would go mad of it; and I believe the physicians really attribute something of the growing prevalence of neurotic disorders to the wear and tear of the nerves from the vivid rush of the trains passing almost momently, and the perpetual jarring of the earth and air from their swift transit. I once spent an evening in one of these apartments, which a friend had taken for a few weeks last spring (you can get them out of the season for any length of time), and as the weather had begun to be warm, we had the windows open, and so we had the full effect of the railroad operated under them. My friend had become accustomed to it, but for me it was an affliction which I cannot give you any notion of. The trains seemed to be in the room with us, and I sat as if I had a locomotive in my lap. Their shrieks and groans burst every sentence I began, and if I had not been master of that visible speech which we use so much at home, I never should have known what my friend was saying. I cannot tell you how this brutal clamor insulted me, and made the mere exchange of thought a part of the squalid struggle which is the plutocratic conception of life; I came away after a few hours of it, bewildered and bruised, as if I had been beaten upon with hammers.

Some of the apartments on the elevated lines are very good, as such things go; they are certainly costly enough to be good; and they are inhabited by people who can afford to leave them during the hot season when the noise is at its worst; but most of them belong to people who must dwell in them summer and winter, for want of money and leisure to get out of them, and who must suffer incessantly from the noise I could not bear for a few hours. In health it is bad enough, but in sickness it must be horrible beyond all parallel. Imagine a mother with a dying child in such a place; or a wife bending over the pillow of her husband to catch the last faint whisper of farewell, as a Harlem train of five or six cars goes roaring by the open window! What horror, what profanation!

The noise is bad everywhere in New York, but in some of the finer apartment houses on the better streets, you are as well out of it as you can be anywhere in the city. I have been a guest in these at different times, and in one of them I am such a frequent guest that I may be said to know its life intimately. In fact, my hostess (women transact society so exclusively in America that you seldom think of your host) in the apartment I mean to speak of, invited me to explore it one night when I dined with her, so that I might, as she said, tell my friends when I got back to Altruria how people lived in America; and I cannot feel that I am violating her hospitality in telling you before

I get back. She is that Mrs. Makely, whom I met last summer in the mountains, and whom you thought so strange a type, but who is not altogether uncommon here. I confess that with all her faults, I like her, and I like to go to her house. She is, in fact, a very good woman, perfectly selfish by tradition as the American women must be, and wildly generous by nature, as they nearly always are; and infinitely superior to her husband in cultivation, as is commonly the case here. As he knows nothing but business, he thinks it the only thing worth knowing, and he looks down on the tastes and interests of her more intellectual life, with amiable contempt, as something almost comic. She respects business, too, and so she does not despise his ignorance as you would suppose; it is at least the ignorance of a business man, who must have something in him beyond her ken, or else he would not be able to make money as he does.

With your greater sense of humor, I think you would be amused if you could see his smile of placid self-satisfaction as he listens to our discussion of questions and problems which no more enter his daily life than they enter the daily life of an Eskimo; but I do not find it altogether amusing myself, and I could not well forgive it, if I did not know that he was at heart so simple and good, in spite of his commerciality. But he *is* sweet and kind, as the American men so often are, and he thinks his wife is the delightfullest creature in the world, as the American husband nearly always does. As a matter of form, he keeps me a little while with him after dinner, when she has left the table, and smokes his cigar, after wondering why we do not smoke in Altruria; but I can see that he is impatient to get to her in their drawing-room, where we find her reading a book in the crimson light of the canopied lamp, and where he presently falls silent, perfectly happy to be near her. The drawing-room is of a good size itself, and it has a room opening out of it, called the library, with a case of books in it, and Mrs. Makely's pianoforte. The place is rather too richly and densely rugged, and there is rather more curtaining and shading of the windows than we should like; but Mrs. Makely is too well up to date, as she would say, to have much of the bric-a-brac about which she tells me used to clutter people's houses here. There are some pretty good pictures on the walls, and a few vases and bronzes, and she says she has produced a greater effect of space by quelling the furniture; she means, having few pieces and having them as small as possible. There is a little stand with her afternoon tea-set in one corner, and there is a pretty writing-desk in the library; I remember a sofa, and some easy chairs, but not too many of them. She has a table near one of the windows, with books and papers on it. She tells me that she sees herself that the place is kept just as she wishes it, for she has rather a passion for neatness, and you never can trust servants not to stand the books on their heads, or study a vulgar symmetry in the arrangements. She never allows them in there, she says, except when they are at work under her eye; and she never allows anybody there except her guests, and her husband after he has smoked. Of course her dog must be there; and one evening after her husband fell asleep in the armchair near her, the dog fell asleep on the fleece at her feet, and we heard them softly breathing in unison.

She made a pretty little mocking mouth when the sound first became audible, and said that she ought really to have sent Mr. Makely out with the dog, for the dog ought to have the air every day, and she had been kept indoors; but sometimes Mr. Makely came home from business so tired that she hated to send him out, even for the dog's sake, though he was so apt to become dyspeptic. "They won't let you have dogs in some of the apartment houses, but I tore up the first lease that had that clause in it, and I told Mr. Makely that I would rather live in a house all my days, than any flat where my dog wasn't as welcome as I was. Of course, they're rather troublesome."

The Makelys had no children, but it is seldom that the occupants of apartment houses of a good class have children, though there is no clause in the lease against them. I verified this fact from Mrs. Makely herself, by actual inquiry, for in all the times that I had gone up and down in the elevator to her apartment, I had never seen any children. She seemed at first to think I was joking, and not to like it, but when she found that I was in earnest, she said that she did not suppose all the families living under that roof had more than four or five children among them. She said that it would be inconvenient; and I could not allege the tenement houses, where children seemed to swarm, for it is but too probable that they do not regard convenience in such places, and that neither parents nor children are more comfortable for their presence.

Comfort is the American ideal, in a certain way, and comfort is certainly what is studied in such an apartment as the Makelys inhabit. We got to talking about it, and the ease of life in such conditions, and it was then she made me that offer to show me her flat, and let me report to the Altrurians concerning it. She is all impulse, and she asked, how would I like to see it *now?* and when I said I should be delighted, she spoke to her husband, and told him that she was going to show me through the flat. He roused himself promptly, and went before us, at her bidding, to turn up the electrics in the passages and rooms, and then she led the way out through the dining-room.

"This and the parlors count three, and the kitchen here is the fourth room of the eight," she said, and as she spoke she pushed open the door of a small room, blazing with light, and dense with the fumes of the dinner and the dishwashing which was now going on in a closet opening out of the kitchen.

She showed me the set range, at one side, and the refrigerator in an alcove, which she said went with the flat, and "Lena," she said to the cook, "this is the Altrurian gentleman I was telling you about, and I want him to see your kitchen. Can I take him into your room?"

The cook said, "Oh, yes, ma'am," and she gave me a good stare, while Mrs. Makely went to the kitchen window, and made me observe that it let in the outside air, though the court that it opened into was so dark that one had to keep the electrics going in the kitchen night and day. "Of course, it's an expense," she said, as she closed the kitchen door after us. She added in a low, rapid tone, "You must excuse my introducing the cook. She has read all about you in the papers—you didn't know, I suppose, that there were reporters, that day of your delightful talk in the mountains, but I had them—and she was wild, when she heard you were coming, and made me promise to let her have a sight of you somehow. She says she wants to go and live in Altruria, and if you would like to take home a cook, or a servant of any kind, you wouldn't have any trouble. Now here," she ran on, without a moment's pause, while she flung open another door, "is what you won't find in every apartment house, even very good ones, and that's a back-elevator. Generally, there are only stairs, and they make the poor things climb the whole way up from the basement, when they come in, and all your marketing has to be brought up that way, too; sometimes they send it up on a kind of dumb-waiter, in the cheap places, and you give your orders to the marketmen down below through a speaking-tube. But here we have none of that bother, and this elevator is for the kitchen and the housekeeping part of the flat. The grocer's and the butcher's man, and anybody who has packages for you, or trunks, or that sort of thing, use it, and, of course, it's for the servants, and they appreciate not having to walk up, as much as anybody."

"Oh, yes," I said, and she shut the elevator door, and opened another a little beyond it.

"This is our guest-chamber," she continued, as she ushered me into a very pretty room, charmingly furnished. "It isn't very light by day, for it opens on a court, like the kitchen and the servants' room here," and with that she whipped out of the guest-chamber and into another doorway, across the corridor. This room was very much narrower, but there were two small beds in it, very neat and clean, with some furnishings that were in keeping, and a good carpet under foot. Mrs. Makely was clearly proud of it, and expected me to applaud it; but I waited for her to speak, which upon the whole she probably liked as well.

"I only keep two servants, because in a flat there isn't really room for more, and I put out the wash and get in cleaning-women when it's needed. I like to use my servants well, because it pays, and I hate to see anybody imposed upon. Some people put in a double-decker, as they call it, a bedstead with two tiers, like the berths on a ship; but I think that's a shame, and I give them two regular beds, even if it does crowd them a little more, and the beds have to be rather narrow. This room has outside air, from the court, and though it's always dark, it's very pleasant, as you see." I did not say that I did not see, and this sufficed for Mrs. Makely.

"Now," she said, "I'll show you *our* rooms," and she flew down the corridor toward two doors that stood open side by side, and flashed into them before me. Her husband was already in the first she entered, smiling in supreme content with his wife, his belongings and himself.

"This is a southern exposure, and it has a perfect gush of sun from morning till night. Some of the flats have the kitchen at the end, and that's stupid; you can have a kitchen in any sort of hole, for you can keep on the electrics, and with them the air is perfectly good. As soon as I saw these chambers, and found out that they would let you keep a dog, I told Mr. Makely to sign the lease instantly, and I would see to the rest."

She looked at me, and I praised the room and its dainty tastefulness to her heart's content, so that she said: "Well, it's some satisfaction to show you anything, Mr. Homos. you are so appreciative. I'm sure you'll give a good account of us to the Altrurians. Well, now we'll go back to the pa—drawing-room. This is the end of the story."

"Well," said her husband, with a wink at me, "I thought it was to be continued in our next," and he nodded toward the door that opened from his wife's bower into the room adjoining.

"Why, you poor old fellow!" she shouted. "I forgot all about *your* room," and she dashed into it before us and began to show it off. It was equipped with every bachelor luxury, and with every appliance for health and comfort. "And here," she said, "he can smoke, or anything, as long as he keeps the door shut. . . . Oh, good gracious! I forgot the bath-room," and they both united in showing me this, with its tiled floor and walls and its porcelain tub; and then Mrs. Makely flew up the corridor before us. "Put out the electrics, Dick!" she called back over her shoulder.

When we were again seated in the drawing-room, which she had been so near calling a parlor, she continued to bubble over with delight in herself and her apartment. "Now, isn't it about perfect?" she urged, and I had to own that it was indeed very convenient and very charming; and in the rapture of the moment, she invited me to criticise it.

"I see very little to criticise," I said, "from your point of view; but I hope you won't think it indiscreet if I ask a few questions?"

She laughed. "Ask anything, Mr. Homos! I hope I got hardened to your questions in the mountains."

"She said you used to get off some pretty tough ones," said her husband, helpless to take his eyes from her, although he spoke to me.

"It is about your servants," I began.

"Oh, of course! Perfectly characteristic! Go on!"

"You told me that they had no natural light either in the kitchen or their bedroom. Do they never see the light of day?"

The lady laughed heartily. "The waitress is in the front of the house several hours every morning at her work, and they both have an afternoon off once a week. Some people only let them go once a fortnight; but I think they are human beings as well as we are, and I let them go *every* week."

"But, except for that afternoon once a week, your cook lives in electric light perpetually?"

"Electric light is very healthy, and it doesn't heat the air!" the lady triumphed. "I can assure you that she thinks she's very well off; and so she is." I felt a little temper in her voice, and I was silent, until she asked me, rather stiffly: "Is there any *other* inquiry you would like to make?"

"Yes," I said, "but I do not think you would like it."

"Now, I assure you, Mr. Homos, you were never more mistaken in your life. I perfectly delight in your naïveté. I know that the Altrurians don't think as we do about some things, and I don't expect it. What is it you would like to ask?"

"Well, why should you require your servants to go down on a different elevator from yourselves?"

"Why, good gracious!" cried the lady. "Aren't they different from us in every way? To be sure they dress up in their ridiculous best when they go out, but you couldn't expect us to let them use the *front* elevator? I don't want to go up and down with my own cook, and I certainly don't with my neighbor's cook!"

"Yes, I suppose you would feel that an infringement of your social dignity. But if you found yourself beside a cook in a horse-car or other public conveyance, you would not feel personally affronted?"

"No, that is a very different thing. That is something we cannot control. But, thank goodness, we *can* control our elevator, and if I were in a house where I had to ride up and down with the servants, I would no more stay in it than I would in one where I couldn't keep a dog. I should consider it a perfect outrage. I cannot understand you, Mr. Homos! You are a gentleman, and you must have the traditions of a gentleman, and yet you ask me such a thing as that!"

I saw a cast in her husband's eye which I took for a hint not to press the matter, and so I thought I had better say, "It is only that in Altruria we hold serving in peculiar honor."

"Well," said the lady scornfully, "if you went and got your servants from an intelligence office, and had to look up their references, you wouldn't hold them in very much honor. I tell you they look out for their own interests as sharply as we do for ours, and it's nothing between us but a question of—"

"Business," suggested her husband.

"Yes," she assented, as if this clinched the matter.

"That's what I'm always telling you, Dolly, and yet you *will* try to make them your friends, as soon as you get them into your house. You want them to love you, and you know that sentiment hasn't got anything to do with it."

"Well, I can't help it, Dick. I can't live with a person without trying to like them, and wanting them to like me. And then, when the ungrateful things are saucy, or leave me in the lurch as they do half the time, it almost breaks my heart. But I'm thankful to say that in these hard times they won't be apt to leave a good place without a good reason."

"Are there many seeking employment?" I asked this because I thought that it was safe ground.

"Well, they just stand around in the offices as *thick!*" said the lady. "And the Americans are trying to get places as well as the foreigners. But I won't have Americans. They are too uppish, and they are never half as well trained as the Swedes or the Irish. They still expect to be treated as one of the family. I suppose," she continued, with a lingering ire in her voice, "that in Altruria, you do treat them as one of the family?"

"We have no servants, in the American sense," I answered as inoffensively as I could.

Mrs. Makely irrelevantly returned to the question that had first provoked her indignation. "And I should like to know how much worse it is to have a back elevator for the servants than it is to have the basement door for the servants, as you always do when you live in a separate house?"

"I should think it was no worse," I admitted, and I thought this a good chance to turn the talk from the dangerous channel it had taken. "I wish, Mrs. Makely, you would tell me something about the way people live in separate houses in New York."

She was instantly pacified. "Why, I should be delighted. I only wish my friend Mrs. Bellington Strange was back from Europe, and I could show you a model house. I mean to take you there, as soon as she gets home. She's a kind of Altrurian herself, you know. She was my dearest friend at school, and it almost broke my heart when she married Mr. Strange, so much older, and her inferior every way. But she's got his money now, and O, the good she does do with it! I know you'll like each other, Mr. Homos. I do wish Eva was at home!"

I said that I should be very glad to meet an American Altrurian, but that now I wished she would tell me about the normal New York house, and what was its animating principle, beginning with the basement door.

She laughed and said, "Why it's just like any other house!"

A. HOMOS.

LETTERS OF AN ALTRURIAN TRAVELLER.

BY W. D. HOWELLS.

PLUTOCRATIC HOUSEKEEPING.

VII.

New York, November 25, 1893.

I CAN never insist enough, my dear Cyril, upon the illogicality of American life. You know what the plutocratic principle is, and what the plutocratic civilization should logically be. But the plutocratic civilization is much better than it should logically be, bad as it is ; for the personal equation constantly modifies it, and renders it far less dreadful than you would reasonably expect. That is, the potentialities of goodness implanted in the human heart by the Creator forbid the plutocratic man to be what the plutocratic scheme of life implies. He is often merciful, kindly and generous, as I have told you already, in spite of conditions absolutely egoistical. You would think that the Americans would be abashed in view of the fact that their morality is often in contravention of their economic principles, but apparently they are not so, and I believe that for the most part they are not aware of the fact. Nevertheless, the fact is there, and you must keep it in mind, if you would conceive of them rightly. You can in no other way account for the contradictions which you will find in my experiences among them ; and these are often so bewildering, that I have to take myself in hand, from time to time, and ask myself what mad world have I fallen into, and whether, after all, it is not a ridiculous nightmare. I am not sure, that when I return, and we talk these things over together, I shall be able to overcome your doubts of my honesty, and I think that when I no longer have them before my eyes, I shall begin to doubt my own memory. But for the present, I can only set down what I at least seem to see, and trust you to accept it, if you cannot understand it.

Perhaps I can aid you by suggesting that, logically, the Americans should be what the Altrurians are, since their polity embodies our belief that all men are born equal, with the right to life, liberty, and the pursuit of happiness ; but that illogically they are what the Europeans are, since they still cling to the economical ideals of Europe, and hold that men are born socially unequal, and deny them the liberty and happiness which can come from equality alone. It is in their public life and civic life that Altruria prevails ;

it is in their social and domestic life that Europe prevails ; and here, I think, is the severest penalty they must pay for excluding women from political affairs ; for women are at once the best and the worst Americans : the best because their hearts are the purest, the worst because their heads are the idlest. "Another contradiction !" you will say, and I cannot deny it ; for with all their cultivation, the American women have no real intellectual interests, but only intellectual fads ; and while they certainly think a great deal, they reflect little, or not at all. The inventions and improvements which have made their household work easy, the wealth that has released them in such vast numbers from work altogether, has not enlarged them to the sphere of duties which our Altrurian women share with us, but has left them, with their quickened intelligences, the prey of the trivialities which engross the European women, and which have formed the life of the sex hitherto in every country where women have an economical and social freedom without the political freedom that can alone give it dignity and import. They have a great deal of beauty, and they are inconsequently charming ; I need not tell you that they are romantic and heroic, or that they would go to the stake for a principle, if they could find one, as willingly as any martyr of the past ; but they have not much more perspective than children, and their reading and their talking about their reading, seem not to have broadened their mental horizons beyond the old sunrise and the old sunset of the kitchen and the parlor.

In fine, the American house as it is, the American household, is what the American woman makes it, and wills it to be, whether she wishes it to be so or not ; for I often find that the American woman wills things that she in nowise wishes. What the normal New York house is, however, I had great difficulty in getting Mrs.

Drawn by Reginald Coxe.

NO REAL INTELLECTUAL INTEREST.

I ASKED MY FRIEND, MR. MAKELY.

Drawn by Reginald Coxe.

Makely to tell me, for, as she said quite frankly, she could not imagine my not knowing. She asked me if I really wanted her to begin at the beginning, and when I said that I did, she took a little more time to laugh at the idea, and then she said: "I suppose you mean a brown-stone, four-story house in the middle of a block?"

"Yes, I think that is what I mean," I said.

"Well," she began, "those high steps that they all have, unless they're English basement-houses, really gives them another story, for people used to dine in the front room of their basements. You've noticed the little front yard, about as big as a handkerchief, generally, and the steps leading down to the iron gate, which is kept locked, and the basement door inside the gate? Well, that's what you might call the back-elevator of a house, for it serves the same purpose: the supplies are brought in there, and marketmen go in and out, and the ashes, and the swill, and the servants—that you object to so much. We have no alleys in New York, the blocks are so narrow, north and south; and, of course, we have no back doors; so we have to put the garbage out on the sidewalk; and it's nasty enough, goodness knows. Underneath the sidewalk, there are bins where people keep their coal and kindling. You've noticed the gratings in the pavements?"

I said yes, and I was ashamed to own that at first I had thought them some sort of registers for tempering the cold in winter; this would have appeared ridiculous in the last degree to my hostess, for the Americans have as yet no conception of publicly modifying the climate, as we do.

"Back of what used to be the dining-room, and what is now used for a laundry, generally, is the kitchen, with closets between, of course, and then the back yard, which some people make very pleasant with shrubs and vines; the kitchen is usually dark and close, and the girls can get a breath of fresh air in the yard; I like to see them; but generally it's taken up with clothes-lines, for people in houses nearly all have their washing done at home. Over the kitchen is the dining-room, which takes up the whole of the first floor, with the pantry, and it almost always has a bay-window out of it; of course, that overhangs the kitchen, and darkens it a little more, but it makes the dining-room so pleasant. I tell my husband that I would be almost willing to live in a house again, just on account of the dining-room bay-window. I had it full of flowers in pots, for the southern sun came in; and then the yard was so nice for the dog; you didn't have to take him out for exercise, yourself; he chased the cats there and got plenty of it. I must say that the cats on the back fences, were a drawback at night; to be sure, we have them here, too; it's seven stories down, but you do hear them, along in the spring. The parlor, or drawing-room, is usually rather long, and runs from the dining-room to the front of the house, though where the house is very deep, they have a sort of middle-room, or back-parlor. Dick, get some paper and draw it! Wouldn't you like to see a plan of the floor?"

I said that I would, and she bade her husband make it like their old house in West Thirty-third. We all looked at it together.

"This is the front door," Mrs. Makely explained, "where people come in, and then begins the misery of a house: *stairs!* They mostly go up straight, but sometimes they have them curve a little, and in the new houses the architects have all sorts of little dodges for squaring them and putting landings. Then on the second floor—draw it, Dick!—you have two nice large chambers, with plenty of light and air, before and behind. I do miss the light and air in a flat, there's no denying it."

"You'll go back to a house yet, Dolly," said her husband.

"Never!" she almost shrieked, and he winked at me, as if it were the best joke in the world. "Never, as long as houses have stairs!"

"Put you in an elevator," he suggested.

"Well, that is what Eveleth Strange has, and she lets the servants use it, too," and Mrs. Makely said, with a look at me: "I suppose that would please *you*, Mr. Homos. Well, there's a nice side-room over the front door here, and a bath-room at the rear. Then you have more stairs, and large chambers, and two side-rooms. That makes plenty of chambers for a small family. I used to give two of the third-story rooms to my two girls. I ought really to have made them sleep in one; it seemed such a shame to let the cook have a whole large room to herself; but I had nothing else to do with it, and she did take such comfort in it, poor old thing. You see, the rooms came wrong in our house, for it fronted north, and I had to give the girls sunny rooms, or else give them front rooms, so that it was as broad as it was long. I declare, I was perplexed about it the whole time we lived there, it seemed so perfectly anomalous."

"And what is an English basement-house like?" I ventured to ask, in interruption of the retrospective melancholy she had fallen into.

"Oh, *never* live in an English basement-house, if you value your spine!" cried the lady. "An English basement-house is nothing *but* stairs. In the first place, it's only one room wide, and it's a story higher than a high-stoop house. It's one room forward and one back, the whole way up; and in an English basement it's always *up*, and *never* down. If I had my way, there wouldn't one stone be left upon another in the English basements in New York."

I have suffered Mrs. Makely to be nearly as explicit to you as she was to me; for the kind of house she described is of the form ordinarily prevailing in all American cities, and you can form some idea from it how city people live here. I ought perhaps to tell you that such a house is fitted with every housekeeping convenience, and that there is hot and cold water throughout, and gas everywhere. It has fireplaces in all the rooms, where fires are often kept burning for pleasure; but it is really heated from a furnace in the basement, through large pipes carried to the different stories, and opening into them by some such registers as we use. The separate houses sometimes have steam-heating, but not often. They each have their drainage into the sewer of the street, and this is trapped and trapped again, as in the houses of our old plutocratic cities, to keep the poison of the sewer from getting into the houses.

You will be curious to know something concerning the cost of living in such a house, and you may be sure that I did not fail to question Mrs. Makely on this point. She was at once very volubly communicative; she told me all she knew, and, as her husband said, "a great deal more."

"Why, of course," she began, "you can spend all you have, in New York, if you like, and people do spend fortunes every year. But I suppose you mean the average cost of living in a brownstone house, in a good block, that rents for $1800 or $2000 a year, with a family of three or four children, and two servants. Well, what should you say, Dick?"

"Ten or twelve thousand a year," answered her husband.

"Yes, fully that," she answered, with an effect of disappointment in his figures. "We had just ourselves, and we never spent less than seven, and we didn't dress, and we didn't entertain, either, to speak of. But you have to live on a certain scale, and generally you live up to your income."

"Quite," said Mr. Makely.

"I don't know what makes it cost

Drawn by Reginald Coxe.
"OFTEN WISHES HE WAS A MASTER-MECHANIC."

so. Provisions are cheap enough, and they say people live in as good style for a third less in London. There used to be a superstition that you could live for less in a flat, and they always talk to you about the cost of a furnace, and a man to tend it, and keep the snow shovelled off your sidewalk, but that is all stuff. Five hundred dollars will make up the whole difference, and more. You pay quite as much rent for a decent flat, and then you don't get half the room. No, if it wasn't for the stairs, I wouldn't live in a flat for an instant. But that makes all the difference."

"And the young people," I urged; "those who are just starting in life, how do they manage? Say when the husband has $1500 or $2500 a year?"

"Poor things!" she returned. "I don't know how they manage. They board, till they go distracted, or they dry up, and blow away; or else the wife has a little money, too; and they take a small flat, and ruin themselves. Of course, they want to live nicely, and like other people."

"But if they didn't?"

"Why, then they could live delightfully. My husband says he often wishes he was a master-mechanic in New York, with a thousand a year, and a flat for twelve dollars a month; he would have the best time in the world."

Her husband nodded his acquiescence. "Fighting-cock wouldn't be in it," he said. "Trouble is, we all want to do the swell thing."

"But you can't all do it," I ventured, "and from what I see of simple, out-of-the-way neighborhoods in my walks, you don't all try."

"Why, no," he said. "Some of us were talking about that the other night at the club, and one of the fellows was saying that he believed there was as much old-fashioned, quiet, almost countrified life in New York, among the great mass of the people, as you'd find in any city in the world. Said you met old codgers that took care of their own furnaces, just as you would in a town of five thousand inhabitants."

"Yes, that's all very well," said his wife. "But they wouldn't be nice people. Nice people want to live nicely. And so they live beyond their means, or else they scrimp and suffer. I don't know which is worst."

"But there is no obligation to do either?" I asked.

"Oh, yes, there is," she returned. "If you've been born in a certain way, and brought up in a certain way, you can't get out of it. You simply can't. You have got to keep in it till you drop. Or a woman has."

"That means the woman's husband, too," said Mr. Makely, with his wink for me. "Always die together."

In fact, there is the same competition in the social world as in the business world; and it is the ambition of every American to live in some such house as the New York house, and as soon as a village begins to grow into a town, such houses are built. Still, the immensely greater number of the Americans necessarily live so simply and cheaply, that such a house would be almost as strange to them as to an Altrurian. But while we should regard its furnishings as vulgar and unwholesome, most Americans would admire and covet its rich rugs or carpets, its papered walls, and thickly curtained windows, and all its foolish ornamentation, and most American women would long to have a house like the ordinary high-stoop New York house, that they might break their backs over its stairs, and become invalids, and have servants about them to harass them and hate them.

Of course, I put it too strongly, for there is often, illogically, a great deal of love between the American women and their domestics, though why there should be any at all I cannot explain, except by reference to that mysterious personal equation which modifies all stations here. You will have made your reflection that the servants, as they are cruelly called, (I have heard them called so in their hearing, and wondered they did not fly tooth and nail at the throat that uttered the insult), form really no part of the house, but are aliens in the household and the family life. In spite of this fact, much kindness grows up between them and the family, and they do not always slight the work that I cannot understand their ever having any heart in. Often they do slight it, and they insist unsparingly upon the scanty privileges which their mistresses seem to think a monstrous invasion of their own rights. The habit of oppression grows upon the oppressor, and you would find tenderhearted women here, gentle friends, devoted wives, loving mothers, who would be willing that their domestics should remain indoors, week in and week out, and, where they are confined in the ridiculous American flat, never see the light of day. In fact, though the Americans do not know it, and would be shocked to be told it, their servants are really slaves, who are none the less slaves, because they cannot be beaten, or bought and sold except by the week or month, and for the price which they fix themselves, and themselves receive in the form of wages. They are social outlaws, so far as the society of the family they serve is concerned, and they are restricted in the visits they receive and pay among themselves. They are given the worst rooms in the house, and they are fed with the food that they have prepared, only when it comes cold from the family table; in the wealthier houses, where many of them are kept, they are supplied a coarser and cheaper victual bought and cooked for them apart from that provided for the family. They are subject at all hours, from six in the morning till any time of night, to the pleasure or caprice of the master or mistress. In fine, every circumstance of their life is an affront to their pride, to that just self-respect which even Americans allow is the right of every human being. With the rich, they are said to be sometimes indolent, dishonest, mendacious, and all that Plato long ago explained that slaves must be; but in the middle-class families they are mostly faithful, diligent, and reliable in a degree that would put to shame most business men who hold positions of trust in the plutocracy, and would leave many ladies whom they relieve of work without ground for comparison.

After Mrs. Makely had told me about the New York house, we began to talk of the domestic service, and I ventured to hint some of the things that I have so plainly said to you. She frankly consented to my whole view of the matter, for if she wishes to make an effect or gain a point, she has a magnanimity that stops at nothing short of self-devotion. "I know it," she said. "You are perfectly right; but here we are, and what are we to do? What do you do in Altruria, I should like to know?"

I said that in Altruria we all worked, and that personal service was as honored among us as medical attendance in America; I did not know what other comparison to make; but that any one in health would think it as unwholesome and as immoral to let another serve him as to let a doctor physic him. At this Mrs. Makely and her husband laughed so that I found myself unable to go on for some moments, till Mrs. Makely, with a final shriek, shouted to him, "Dick, do stop, or I shall die! Excuse me, Mr. Homos, but you are so deliciously funny, and I know you're just joking. You *won't* mind my laughing. Do go on!"

I tried to give her some notion as to how we manage, in our common life, which we have simplified so much beyond anything that this barbarous people dream of; and she grew a little soberer as I went on, and seemed at least to believe that, as her husband said, I was not stuffing them; but she ended, as they always do here, by saying that it might be all very well in Altruria, but it would never do in America, and that it was contrary to human nature to have so many things done in common. "Now, I'll tell you," she said. "After we broke up housekeeping in Thirty-third street, we stored our furniture—"

"Excuse me!" I said. "How, stored?"

"Oh, I dare say you never store your furniture in Altruria. But here we have hundreds of storehouses of all sorts and sizes, packed with furniture that people put into them when they go to Europe, or get sick to death of servants and the whole bother of housekeeping; and that's what we did; and, then, as my husband says, we browsed about for a year or two. First, we tried hotelling it, and we took a hotel apartment furnished, and dined at the hotel table, until I certainly thought I should go off, I got so tired of it. Then, we hired a suite in one of the family hotels that there are so many of, and got out enough of our things to furnish it, and had our meals in our rooms; they let you do that for the same price, often they are *glad* to have you, for the dining-room is so packed. But everything got to tasting just the same as everything else, and my husband had the dyspepsia so bad he couldn't half attend to business, and I suffered from indigestion myself, cooped up in a few small rooms, that way; and the dog almost died; and finally, we gave that up, and took an apartment, and got out our things—the storage cost as much as the rent of a small house—and put them into it, and had a caterer send in the meals, as they do in Europe. But it isn't the same here as it is in Europe, and we got so sick of it in a month that I thought I should scream when I saw the same old dishes coming on the table, day after day.

Drawn by Reginald Coxe.
THE KITCHEN WINDOW.

We had to keep one servant—excuse me, Mr. Homos; *domestic*—anyway, to look after the table and the parlor and chamber work, and my husband said we might as well be hung for a sheep as a lamb, and so we got in a cook; and bad as it is, it's twenty million times better than anything else you can do. Servants are a plague, but you have got to have them, and so I have resigned myself to the will of Provi-dence. If they don't like it, neither do I, and so I fancy it's about as broad as it's long." I have found this is a favorite phrase of Mrs. Makely's, and that it seems to give her a great deal of comfort.

"And you don't feel that there's any harm in it?" I ventured to ask.

"Harm in it?" she repeated. "Why, aren't the poor things glad to get the work? What would they do without it?"

"From what I see of your conditions I should be afraid that they would starve," I said.

"Yes, they can't all get places in shops or restaurants, and they have to do something, or starve, as you say," she said; and she seemed to think what I had said was a concession to her position.

"But if it were your own case?" I suggested. "If you had no alternatives but starvation and domestic service, you would think there was harm in it, even although you were glad to take a servant's place?"

I saw her flush, and she answered haughtily, "You must excuse me if I refuse to imagine myself taking a servant's place, even for the sake of argument."

"And you are quite right," I said. "Your American instinct is too strong to brook even in imagination the indignities which seem daily, hourly and momently inflicted upon servants in your system."

To my great astonishment she seemed delighted by this conclusion. "Yes," she said, and she smiled radiantly, "and now you understand how it is that American girls won't go out to service, though the pay is so much better and they are so much better housed and fed; and everything. Besides," she added, with an irrelevance which always amuses her husband, though I should be alarmed by it for her sanity if I did not find it so characteristic of women here, who seem to be mentally characterized by the illogicality of the civilization, "they're not half so good as the foreign servants, even when you can get them. They've been brought up in homes of their own, and they're uppish, and they have no idea of anything but third-rate boarding-house cooking, and they're always hoping to get married, so that, really, you have no peace of your life with them."

"And it never seems to you that the whole relation is wrong?" I asked.

"What relation?"

"That between maid and mistress, the hirer and the hireling."

"Why, good gracious!" she burst out. "Didn't Christ himself say that the laborer was worthy of his hire? And how would you get your work done, if you didn't pay for it?"

"It might be done for you, when you could not do it yourself, from affection."

"From affection!" she returned, with the deepest derision. "Well, I rather think I *shall* have to do it myself if I want it done from affection! But I suppose you think I *ought* to do it myself, as the Altrurian ladies do? I can tell you that in America it would be impossible for a lady to do her own work, and there are no intelligence offices where you can find girls that want to work for love. It's as broad as it's long."

"It's simply business," said her husband.

They were right, my dear Cyril, and I was wrong, strange as it must appear to you. The tie of service, which we think as sacred as the tie of blood, can be here only a business relation, and in these conditions service must forever be grudgingly given and grudgingly paid. There is something in it, I do not quite know what, for I can never place myself precisely in an American's place, that degrades the poor creatures who serve, so that they must not only be social outcasts, but must leave such a taint of dishonor on their work, that one cannot even do it for oneself without a sense of outraged dignity. You might account for this in Europe, where ages of prescriptive wrong have distorted the relation out of all human wholesomeness and Christian loveliness; but in America, where many, and perhaps most, of those who keep servants and call them so, are but a single generation from fathers who earned their bread by the sweat of their brows, and from mothers who nobly served in all household offices, it is in the last degree bewildering. I can only account for it by that bedevilment of the entire American ideal through the retention of the English economy when the English polity was rejected. But at the heart of America there is this ridiculous contradiction, and it must remain there until the whole country is Altrurianized. There is no other hope; but I did not now urge this point, and we turned to talk of other things, related to the matters we had been discussing.

"The men," said Mrs. Makely, "get out of the whole bother very nicely, as long as they are single, and even when they're married, they are apt to run off to the club, when there's a prolonged upheaval in the kitchen."

"*I* don't, Dolly," suggested her husband.

"No, *you* don't, Dick," she returned, fondly. "But there are not many like you."

He went on, with a wink at me: "I never live at the club, except in summer, when you go away to the mountains."

"Well, you know I can't very well take you with me," she said.

"Oh, I couldn't leave my business, anyway," he said, and he laughed.

I had noticed the vast and splendid club-houses in the best places in the city, and I had often wondered about their life, which seemed to me a blind groping towards our own, though only upon terms that forbade it to those who most needed it. The clubs here are not like our groups, the free associations of sympathetic people, though one is a little more literary, or commercial, or scientific, or political than another; but the entrance to each is more or less jealously guarded; there is an initiation fee, and there are annual dues, which are usually heavy enough to exclude all but the professional and business classes, though there are, of course, successful artists and authors in them. During the past winter I visited some of the most characteristic, where I dined and supped with the members, or came alone when one of these put me down, for a fortnight or a month.

They are equipped with kitchens and cellars, and their wines and dishes are of the best. Each is, in fact, like a luxurious private house on a large scale; outwardly they are palaces, and inwardly they have every feature and function of a princely residence complete, even to a certain number of guest-chambers, where members may pass the night, or stay indefinitely, in some cases, and actually live at the club. The club, however, is known only to the cities and the larger towns, in this highly developed form; to the ordinary, simple American, of the country, or of the country town of five or ten thousand people, a New York club would be as strange as it would be to any Altrurian.

"Do many of the husbands left behind in the summer live at the clubs?" I asked.

"All that *have* a club, do," he said. "Usually, there's a very good table d'hôte dinner that you couldn't begin to get for the same price anywhere else; and there are a lot of good fellows there, and you can come pretty near forgetting that you're homeless, or even that you're married."

He laughed, and his wife said: "You ought to be ashamed, Dick; and me worrying about you all the time I'm away, and wondering what the cook gives you here. Yes," she continued, addressing me, "that's the worst thing about the clubs. They make the men so comfortable that they say it's one of the principal obstacles to early marriages. The young men try to get lodgings near them, so that they can take their meals there, and they know they get much better things to eat than they could have in a house of their own at a great deal more expense, and so they simply don't think of getting married. Of course," she said with that wonderful, unintentional, or at least unconscious, frankness of hers, "I don't blame the clubs altogether. There's no use denying that girls are expensively brought up, and that a young man has to think twice before taking one of them out of the kind of home she's used to, and putting her into the kind of home he can give her. I suppose it's as broad as it's long. If the clubs have killed early marriages, the women have created the clubs."

"Do women go much to them?" I asked, choosing this question as a safe one.

"*Much!*" she screamed. "They don't go at all! They *can't!* They won't *let* us! To be sure, there are some that have rooms where ladies can go with their friends who are members, and have lunch or dinner; but as for seeing the inside of the club-house proper, where these great creatures"—she indicated her husband—"are sitting up, smoking and telling stories, it isn't to be dreamed of."

Her husband laughed. "You wouldn't like the smoking, Dolly."

"Nor the stories, either, some of them," she retorted.

"Oh, the stories are always first rate," he said, and he laughed more than before.

"And they never gossip, at the clubs, Mr. Homos, never!" she added.

"Well, hardly ever," said her husband, with an intonation that I did not understand. It seemed to be some sort of catch-phrase.

"All I know," said Mrs. Makely, "is that I like to have my husband belong to his club. It's a nice place for him in summer; and very often in winter, when I'm dull, or going out somewhere that he hates, he can go down to his club, and smoke a cigar, and come home just about the time I get in, and it's much better than worrying through the evening with a book. He hates books, poor Dick!" She looked fondly at him, as if this were one of the greatest merits in the world. "But I must confess, I shouldn't like him to be a mere club man, like some of them."

"But how?" I asked.

"Why, belonging to five or six, or more, even; and spending their whole time at them, when they're not at business."

There was a pause, and Mr. Makely put on an air of modest worth, which he carried off with his usual wink toward me. I said, finally, "And if the ladies are not admitted to the men's clubs, why don't they have clubs of their own?"

"Oh, they have,—several, I believe. But who wants to go and meet a lot of women? You meet enough of them in society, goodness knows. You hardly meet any one else, especially at afternoon teas. They bore you to death."

Mrs. Makely's nerves seemed to lie in the direction of a prolongation of this subject, and I asked my next question a little away from it. "I wish you would tell me, Mrs. Makely, something about your way of provisioning your household. You said that the grocer's and butcher's man came up to the kitchen with your supplies—"

"Yes, and the milkman and the iceman; the iceman always puts the ice into the refrigerator; it's very convenient, and quite like your own house."

"But you go out and select the things yourself, the day before, or in the morning?"

"Oh, not at all! The men come and the cook gives the order; she knows pretty well what we want on the different days, and I never meddle with it from one week's end to the other, unless we have friends. The tradespeople send in their bills at the end of the month, and that's all there is of it." Her husband gave me one of his queer looks, and she went on: "When we were younger, and just beginning housekeeping, I used to go out and order the things myself; I used even to go to the big markets, and half kill myself, trying to get things a little cheaper at one place than another, and waste more car-fare, and lay up more doctor's bills than it would all come to, ten times over. I used to fret my life out, remembering the prices; but now, thank goodness, that's all over. I don't know any more what beef is a pound than my husband does; if a thing isn't good, I send it straight back, and that puts them on their honor, you know, and they have to give me the best of everything. The bills average about the same, from month to month; a little more if we have company; but if they're too outrageous, I make a fuss with the cook, and she scolds the men, and then it goes better for a while. Still, it's a great bother."

I confess that I did not see what the bother was, but I had not the courage to ask, for I had already conceived a wholesome dread of the mystery of an American lady's nerves. So I merely suggested, "And that is the way that people usually manage?"

"Why," she said, "I suppose that some old-fashioned people still do their marketing, and people that have to look to their outgoes, and know what every mouthful costs them. But their lives are not worth having. Eveleth Strange does it—or she did do it when she was in the country; I dare say she won't when she gets back—just from a sense of duty, and because she says that a housekeeper ought to know about her expenses. But I ask her who will care whether she knows or not; and as for giving the money to the poor that she saves by spending economically, I tell her that the butchers and the grocers have to live, too, as well as the poor, and so it's as broad as it's long."

I could not make out whether Mr. Makely approved of his wife's philosophy or not; I do not believe he thought much about it. The money probably came easily with him, and he let it go easily, as an American likes to do. There is nothing penurious or sordid about this curious people, so fierce in the pursuit of riches. When these are once gained, they seem to have no value to the man who has won them, and he has generally no object in life but to see his womankind spend them.

This is the season of the famous Thanksgiving, which has now become the national holiday, but has no longer any savor in it of the grim Puritanism it sprang from. It is now appointed by the president and the governors of the several States, in proclamations enjoining a pious gratitude upon the people for their continued prosperity as a nation and a public acknowledgment of the divine blessings. The blessings are supposed to be of the material sort, grouped in the popular imagination as good times, and it is hard to see what they are in these days of adversity, when hordes of men and women of every occupation are feeling the pinch of poverty in their different degree. It is not merely those who have always the wolf at their doors, who are now suffering, but those whom the wolf never threatened before; those who amuse, as well as those who serve the rich, are alike anxious and fearful, where they are not already in actual want; thousands of poor players, as well as hundreds of thousands of poor laborers, are out of employment; and the winter threatens to be one of dire misery. Yet you would not imagine from the smiling face of things, as you would see it in the better parts of this great city, that there was a heavy heart or an empty stomach anywhere below it. In fact, people here are so used to seeing other people in want that it no longer affects them as reality, it is merely dramatic, or hardly so lifelike as that; it is merely histrionic. It is rendered still more spectacular to the imaginations of the fortunate by the melodrama of charity they are invited to take part in by endless appeals, and their fancy is flattered by the notion that they are curing the distress they are only slightly relieving by a gift from their superfluity. The charity, of course, is better than nothing, but it is a fleeting mockery of the trouble at the best. If it were proposed that the city should subsidize a theater at which the idle players could get employment in producing good plays at a moderate cost to the people, the notion would not be considered more ridiculous than that of founding municipal works for the different sorts of idle workers; and it would not be thought half so nefarious, for the proposition to give work by the collectivity is supposed to be in contravention of the sacred principle of monopolistic competition so dear to the American economist, and it would be denounced as an approximation to the surrender of the city to anarchism and destruction by dynamite.

But as I have so often said, the American life is in nowise logical, and you will not be surprised, though you may be shocked or amused to learn that the festival of Thanksgiving is now so generally devoted to witnessing a game of foot-ball between the Elevens of two great universities, that the services at the churches are very scantily attended. The Americans are practical, if they are not logical, and this preference of foot-ball to prayer and praise on Thanksgiving day has gone so far that now a principal church in the city holds its services on Thanksgiving eve, so that the worshippers may not be tempted to keep away from their favorite game.

There is always a heavy dinner at home after the game, to console the friends of those who have lost, and to heighten the joy of the winning side, among the comfortable people. The poor recognize the day largely as a sort of carnival. They go about in masquerade on the eastern avenues, and the children of the foreign races who populate that quarter, penetrate the better streets, blowing horns, and begging of the passers. They have probably no more sense of its difference from the old carnival of catholic Europe than from the still older Saturnalia of pagan times. Perhaps you will say that a masquerade is no more pagan than a foot-ball game; and I confess that I have a pleasure in that innocent misapprehension of the holiday on the East side. I am not more censorious of it than I am of the displays of festival cheer at the provision stores, or green-groceries throughout the city at this time. They are almost as numerous on the avenues as the drinking

Drawn by Reginald Coxe
GOOD NIGHT!

saloons, and thanks to them, the wasteful housekeeping is at least convenient in a high degree. The waste is inevitable with the system of separate kitchens, and it is not in provisions alone, but in labor and in time, a hundred cooks doing the work of one; but the Americans have no conception of our coöperative housekeeping, and so the folly goes on. Meantime, the provision stores add much to their effect of crazy gayety on the avenues.

The variety and harmony of color is very great, and this morning I stood so long admiring the arrangement in one of them, that I am afraid I rendered myself a little suspicious to the policeman guarding the liquor store on the nearest corner; there seems always to be a policeman assigned to this duty. The display was on either side of the provisioner's door, and began on one hand with a basal line of pumpkins well out on the sidewalk. Then it was built up with the soft white and cool green of cauliflowers, and open boxes of red and white grapes, to the window that flourished in banks of celery and rosy apples. On the other side, gray-green squashes formed the foundation, and the wall was sloped upward with the delicious salads you can find here, the dark red of beets, the yellow of carrots, and the blue of cabbages. The association of colors was very artistic and even the line of mutton carcases overhead, with each a brace of grouse, or half a dozen quail in its embrace, and flanked with long sides of beef at the four ends of the line, was picturesque, though the sight of the carnage at the provision stores here would always be dreadful to an Altrurian; in the great markets it is intolerable. This sort of business is mostly in the hands of the Germans, who have a good eye for such effects as may be studied in it; but the fruiterers are nearly all Italians, and their stalls are charming. I always like, too, the cheeriness of the chestnut and peanut ovens of the Italians; the pleasant smell and friendly smoke that rise from them suggest a simple and homelike life, which there are so many things in this great, weary, heedless city to make one forget.

A. HOMOS.

LETTERS OF AN ALTRURIAN TRAVELLER.

BY W. D. HOWELLS.

DINNER, VERY INFORMALLY.

VIII.

New York, December 1, 1893.

My dear Cyril:

I did not suppose that I should be writing you so soon again, but I was out for my first dinner of the season, last night, and I must try to give you my impressions of it while they are still fresh. Only the day after I posted my last letter, I received the note which I enclose:

My dear Mr. Homos:

Will you give me the pleasure of your company, at dinner, on Thanksgiving Day, at eight o'clock, very informally. My friend, Mrs. Bellington Strange, has unexpectedly returned from Europe, within the week, and I am asking a few friends, whom I can trust to excuse this very short notice, to meet her.

With Mr. Makely's best regards,
Yours cordially,
Dorothea Makely.

The Sphinx,
November the twenty-sixth,
Eighteen hundred and
Ninety-three.

I must explain to you that it has been a fad with the ladies here to spell out their dates, and though the fashion is waning, Mrs. Makely is a woman who would remain in such an absurdity among the very last. I will let you make your own conclusions concerning her, for though, as an Altrurian, I cannot respect her, I like her so much, and I have so often enjoyed her generous hospitality, that I cannot bring myself to criticise her except by the implication of the facts. She is anomalous, but to our way of thinking, all the Americans I have met are anomalous, and she has the merits that you would not logically attribute to her character. Of course, I cannot feel that her evident regard for me is the least of these, though I like to think that it is more founded in reason than the rest.

I have by this time become far too well versed in the polite insincerities of the plutocratic world to imagine, that because she asked me to come to her dinner, very informally, I was not to come in all the state I could put into my dress. You know what the evening dress of men is, here, from the costumes in our museum, and you can well believe that I never put on those ridiculous black trousers without a sense of their grotesqueness, that scrap of waistcoat reduced to a mere rim, so as to show the whole white breadth of the starched shirt bosom, and that coat chopped away till it seems nothing but tails and lapels. It is true that I might go out to dinner in our national costume; in fact, Mrs. Makely has often begged to me to wear it, for she says the Chinese wear theirs; but I have not cared to make the sensation which I must if I wore it; my outlandish views of life, and my frank study of theirs signalize me quite sufficiently among the Americans.

At the hour named, I appeared at Mrs. Makely's drawing-room in all the formality that I knew her invitation, to come very informally, really meant. I found myself the first, as I nearly always do, but I had only time for a word or two with my hostess before the others began to come. She hastily explained that as soon as she knew Mrs. Strange was in New York, she had dispatched a note telling her that I was still here; and that as she could not get settled in time to dine at home, she must come and take Thanksgiving with her. "She will have to go out with Mr. Makely; but I am going to put you next to her at table, for I want you both to have a good time. But don't you forget that you are going to take *me* out." I said that I should certainly not forget it, and I showed her the envelope with my name on the outside, and hers on a card inside, which the serving man at the door had given me in the hall, as the first token, after her letter, that the dinner was to be in the last degree unceremonious. She laughed, and said: "I've had the luck to pick up two or three other agreeable people that I know will be glad to meet you. Usually, it's such a scratch lot at Thanksgiving, for everybody dines at home that can, and you have to trust to the highways and the byways for your guests, if you give a dinner. But I did want to bring Mrs. Strange and you together, and so I chanced it. Of course, it's a sent-in dinner, as you must have inferred from the man at the door; I've given my servants a holiday, and had Claret's people do the whole thing. It's as broad as it's long, and as my husband says, you might as well be hung for a sheep as a lamb; and it saves bother. Everybody will know it's sent in, so that nobody will be deceived. There'll be a turkey in it somewhere, and cranberry sauce; I've insisted on that: but it won't be a regular American Thanksgiving dinner, and I'm rather sorry, on your account, for I wanted you to see one, and I meant to have had you here, just with ourselves; but Eveleth Strange's coming back put a new face on things, and so I've gone in for this affair, which isn't at all what you would like. That's the reason I tell you at once, it's sent in."

I am so often at a loss for the connection in Mrs. Makely's ideas that I am more patient with her incoherent jargon than you will be, I am afraid. It went on to much the effect that I have tried to report, until the moment she took the hand of the guest who came next. They arrived, until there were eight of us in all; Mrs. Strange coming last, with excuses for being late. I had somehow figured her as a person rather mystical and recluse in appearance, perhaps on account of her name, and I had imagined her tall and superb. But she was, really, rather small, though not below the woman's average, and she had a face more round than otherwise, with a sort of businesslike earnestness, but a very charming smile, and presently, as I saw, an American sense of humor. She had brown hair and gray eyes, and teeth not too regular to be monotonous; her mouth was very sweet, whether she laughed, or sat gravely silent.

She at once affected me like a person who had been sobered beyond her nature by responsibilities, and had steadily strengthened under the experiences of life. She was dressed with a sort of personal taste, in a rich gown of black lace, which came up to her throat; and she did not subject me to that embarrassment I always feel in the presence of a lady who is much décolleté, when I sit next her, or face to face with her: I cannot always look at her without a sense of taking an immodest advantage. Sometimes I find a kind of pathos in this sacrifice to fashion, as if the poor lady were wearing that sort of gown because she thought she really ought, and then I keep my eyes firmly on hers, or avert them altogether; but there are other cases which have not this appealing quality. Yet in the very worst of the cases it would be a mistake to suppose that there was a display personally meant of the display personally made. Even then it would be found that the gown was worn so because the dressmaker had made it so, and, whether she had made it in this country or in Europe, that she had made it in compliance with a European custom. In fact, all the society customs of the Americans follow some European original, and usually some English original; and it is only fair to say that in this particular custom they do not go to the English extreme.

We did not go out to dinner at Mrs. Makely's by the rules of English precedence, because there are nominally no ranks here, and we could not; but I am sure it will not be long before the Americans will begin playing at precedence just as they now play at the other forms of aristocratic society. For the present, however, there was nothing for us to do but to proceed, when dinner was served, in such order as offered itself, after Mr. Makely gave his arm to Mrs. Strange, though, of course, the white shoulders of the other ladies went gleaming out before the white shoulders of Mrs. Makely shone beside my black ones. I have now become so used to these observances that they no longer affect me as they once did, and as I suppose my account of them must affect you, painfully, comically. But I have always the sense of having a part in amateur theatricals, and I do not see how the Americans can fail to have the same sense, for there is nothing spontaneous in them, and nothing that has grown even dramatically out of their own life.

Often when I admire the perfection of the mise en scène, it is with a vague feeling that I am derelict in not offering it an explicit applause. In fact, this is permitted in some sort and measure, as now when we sat down at Mrs. Makely's exquisite table, and the ladies frankly recognized her touch in it. One of them found a phrase for it at once, and pronounced it a symphony in chrysanthemums; for the color and the character of these flowers played through all the appointment of the table, and rose to a magnificent finale in the vast group in the middle of the board, infinite in their caprices of dye and design. Another lady said that it was a dream, and then Mrs. Makely said: "No, a memory," and confessed that she had studied the effect from her recollection of some tables at a chrysanthemum show held here last year, which seemed failures because they were so simply and crudely adapted in the china and napery to merely one kind and color of the flower.

"Then," she added, "I wanted to do something very chrysanthemummy, because it seems to me the Thanksgiving flower, and belongs to Thanksgiving quite as much as holly belongs to Christmas."

Everybody applauded her intention, and we hungrily fell to upon the excellent oysters, with her warning that we had better make the most of everything in its turn, for she had conformed her dinner to the brevity of the notice she had given her guests.

Just what the dinner was I will try to tell you, for I think that it will interest you to know what people here think a very simple dinner. That is, people of any degree of fashion; for the unfashionable Americans, who are innumerably in the majority, have no more than the Altrurians seen such a dinner as Mrs. Makely's. This sort generally sit down to a single dish of meat, with two or three vegetables, and they drink tea or coffee, or water only, with their dinner. Even when they have company, as they say, the things are all put on the table at once; and the average of Americans who have seen a dinner served in courses, after the Russian manner, invariable in the fine world here, is not greater than those who have seen a serving-man in livery. Among these the host piles up his guest's plate with meat and vegetables, and it is passed from hand to hand till it reaches him; his drink arrives from the hostess by the same means. One maid serves the table in a better class, and two maids in a class still better; it is only when you reach people of very decided form that you find a man in a black coat behind your chair; Mrs. Makely, mindful of the informality of her dinner in everything, had two men.

I should say the difference between the Altrurians and the unfashionable Americans, in view of such a dinner as she gave us, would be that, while it would seem to us abominable for its extravagance, and revolting in its appeals to appetite, it would seem to most of such Americans altogether admirable and enviable, and would appeal to their ambition to give such a dinner themselves as soon as ever they could.

Well, with our oysters, we had a delicate French wine, though I am told that formerly Spanish wines were served. A delicious soup followed the oysters, and then we had fish, with sliced cucumbers dressed with oil and vinegar, like a salad; and I suppose you will ask what we could possibly have eaten more. But this was only the beginning, and next there came a course of sweetbreads with green peas. With this the champagne began at once to flow, for Mrs. Makely was nothing if not original, and she had champagne very promptly. One of the gentlemen praised her for it, and said you could not have it too soon, and he had secretly hoped it would have begun with the oysters. Next, we had a remove, a tenderloin of beef, with mushrooms, fresh, and not of the canned sort which it is usually accompanied with. This fact won our hostess more compliments from the gentlemen, which could not have gratified her more if she had dressed and cooked the dish herself. She insisted upon our trying the stewed terrapin, for if it did come in a little by the neck and shoulders, it was still in place at a Thanksgiving dinner, because it was so American; and the stuffed peppers, which, if they were not American, were at least Mexican, and originated in the kitchen of a sister republic. There were one or two other side-dishes, and with all the burgundy began to be poured out.

Mr. Makely said that claret all came now from California, no matter what French château they named it after, but burgundy you could not err in. His guests were now drinking the different wines, and to much the same effect, I should think, as if they had mixed them all in one cup; though I ought to say that several of the ladies took no wine, and kept me in countenance after the first taste that I was obliged to take of each, in order to pacify my host.

You must know that all the time there were plates of radishes, olives, celery, and roasted almonds set about that every one ate of without much reference to the courses. The talking and the feasting were at their height, but there was a little flagging of the appetite, perhaps, when it received the stimulus of a water-ice flavored with rum. After eating it, I immediately experienced an extraordinary revival of my hunger (I am ashamed to confess that I was gorging myself like the rest), but I quailed inwardly when one of the men-servants set down before Mr. Makely, a roast turkey that looked as large as an ostrich. It was received with cries of joy, and one of the gentlemen said, "Ah, Mrs. Makely, I was waiting to see how you would interpolate the turkey, but you never fail. I knew you would get it in somewhere. But where," he added in a burlesque whisper, behind his hand, "are the—"

"Canvasback duck?" she asked, and at that moment the servant set before the anxious inquirer a platter of these renowned birds, which you know something of already from the report our emissaries have given of their cult among the Americans.

Every one laughed, and after the gentleman had made a despairing flourish over them with a carving knife in emulation of Mr. Makely's emblematic attempt upon the turkey, both were taken away, and carved at a sideboard. They were then served in slices, the turkey with cranberry sauce, and the ducks with currant jelly; and I noticed that no one took so much of the turkey that he could not suffer himself to be helped also to the duck. I must tell you that there was a salad with the duck, and after that there was an ice-cream, with fruit and all manner of candied fruits, and candies, different kinds of cheese, coffee, and liqueurs to drink after the coffee.

"Well, now," Mrs. Makely proclaimed, in high delight with her triumph, "I must let you imagine the pumpkin pie. I meant to have it, because it isn't really Thanksgiving without it. But I couldn't, for the life of me, see where it would come in."

This made them all laugh, and they began to talk about the genuine American character of the holiday, and what a fine thing it was to have something truly national. They praised Mrs. Makely for thinking of so many American dishes, and the facetious gentleman said that she rendered no greater tribute than was due to the overruling Providence which had so abundantly bestowed them upon the Americans as a people. "You must have been glad, Mrs. Strange," he said, to the lady at my side, "to get back to our American oysters. There seems nothing else so potent to bring us home from Europe."

"I'm afraid," she answered, "that I don't care so much for the American oyster as I should. But I am certainly glad to get back."

"In time for the turkey, perhaps?"

"No, I care no more for the turkey than for the oyster of my native land," said the lady.

"Ah, well, say the canvasback duck then. The canvasback duck is no alien. He is as thoroughly American as the turkey, or as any of us."

"No, I should not have missed him, either," persisted the lady.

"What could one have missed," the gentleman said, with a bow to the hostess, "in the dinner Mrs. Makely has given us? If there had been nothing, I should not have missed it," and when the laugh at his drolling had subsided, he asked Mrs. Strange: "Then, if it is not too indiscreet, might I inquire what in the world has lured you again to our shores, if it was not the oyster, nor the turkey, nor yet the canvasback."

"The American dinner-party," said the lady, with the same burlesque.

"Well," he consented, "I think I understand you. It is different from the

English dinner-party in being a festivity rather than a solemnity; though after all the American dinner is only a condition of the English dinner. Do you find us much changed, Mrs. Strange?"

"I think we are every year a little more European," said the lady. "One notices it on getting home."

"I supposed we were so European already," returned the gentleman, "that a European landing among us would think he had got back to his starting point in a sort of vicious circle. I am myself so thoroughly Europeanized in all my feelings and instincts, that do you know, Mrs. Makely, if I may confess it without offence—"

"Oh, by all means!" cried the hostess.

"When that vast bird which we have been praising, that colossal roast turkey, appeared, I felt a shudder go through my delicate substance, such as a refined Englishman might have experienced at the sight, and I said to myself, quite as if I were not one of you, 'Good heavens! now they will begin talking through their noses and eating with their knives. It's what I might have expected!'"

It was impossible not to feel that this gentleman was talking at me; if the Americans have a foreign guest, they always talk at him more or less; and I was not surprised when he said, "I think our friend, Mr. Homos, will conceive my fine revolt from the crude period of our existence which the roast turkey marks as distinctly as the *graffiti* of the cave-dweller proclaim his epoch."

"No," I protested, "I am afraid that I have not the documents for the interpretation of your emotion. I hope you will take pity on my ignorance, and tell me just what you mean."

The others said they none of them knew either, and would like to know, and the gentleman began by saying that he had been going over the matter in his mind on his way to dinner, and he had really been trying to lead up to it ever since we sat down. "I've been struck, first of all, by the fact, in our evolution, that we haven't socially evolved from ourselves; we've evolved from the Europeans, from the English. I don't think you'll find a single society rite with us now that had its origin in our peculiar national life, if we have a peculiar national life; I doubt it, sometimes. If you begin with the earliest thing in the day, if you begin with breakfast, as society gives breakfasts, you have an English breakfast, though American people and provisions."

"I must say, I think they're both much nicer," said Mrs. Makely.

"Ah, there I am with you! We borrow the form, but we infuse the spirit. I am talking about the form, though. Then, if you come to the society lunch, which is almost indistinguishable from the society breakfast, you have the English lunch, which is really an undersized English dinner. The afternoon tea is English again, with its troops of eager females and stray, reluctant males; though I believe there are rather more men at the English teas, owing to the larger leisure class in England. The afternoon tea and the "at home" are as nearly alike as the breakfast and the lunch. Then, in the course of time, we arrive at the great society function, the dinner; and what is the dinner with us but the dinner of our mother-country?"

"It is livelier," suggested Mrs. Makely, again.

"Livelier, I grant you, but I am still speaking of the form, and not of the spirit. The evening reception, which is gradually fading away, as a separate rite, with its supper and its dance, we now have as the English have it, for the people who have not been asked to dinner. The ball, which brings us round to breakfast again, is again the ball of our Anglo-Saxon kin beyond the seas. In short, from the society point of view we are in everything their mere rinsings."

"Nothing of the kind!" cried Mrs. Makely. "I won't let you say such a thing! On Thanksgiving Day, too! Why, there is the Thanksgiving dinner itself! If that isn't purely American, I should like to know what is."

"It is purely American, but it is strictly domestic; it is not society. Nobody but some great soul like you, Mrs. Makely, would have the courage to ask anybody to a Thanksgiving dinner, and even you ask only such easy-going house-friends as we are proud to be. You wouldn't think of giving a dinner-party on Thanksgiving?"

"No, I certainly shouldn't. I should think it was very presuming; and you are all as nice as you can be to have come to-day; I am not the only great soul at the table. But that is neither here nor there. Thanksgiving is a purely American thing, and it's more popular than ever. A few years ago you never heard of it outside of New England."

The gentleman laughed. "You are perfectly right, Mrs. Makely, as you always are. Thanksgiving is purely American. So is the corn-husking, so is the apple-bee, so is the sugar-party, so is the spelling-match, so is the church-sociable; but none of these have had their evolution in our society entertainments. The New Year's call was also purely American, but that is now as extinct as the dodo, though I believe the other American festivities are still known in the rural districts."

"Yes," said Mrs. Makely, "and I think it's a great shame that we can't have some of them in a refined form in society. I once went to a sugar-party up in New Hampshire, when I was a girl, and I never enjoyed myself so much in my life. I should like to make up a party to go to one somewhere in the Catskills, in March, Will you all go? It would be something to show Mr. Homos. I should like to show him something really American before he goes home. There's nothing American left in society!"

"You forget the American woman," suggested the gentleman. "She is always American, and she is always in society."

"Yes," returned our hostess, with a thoughtful air, "you're quite right in that. One always meets more women than men in society. But it's because the men are so lazy, and so comfortable at their clubs, they won't go. They enjoy themselves well enough in society after they get there, as I tell my husband, when he grumbles over having to dress."

"Well," said the gentleman, "a great many things, the day-time things, we really can't come to, because we don't belong to the aristocratic class, as you ladies do, and we are busy down town. But I don't think we are reluctant about dinner; and the young fellows are nearly always willing to go to a ball, if the supper's good, and it's a house where they don't feel obliged to dance. But what do *you* think, Mr. Homos?" he asked. "How does your observation coincide with my experience?"

I answered that I hardly felt myself qualified to speak, for though I had assisted at the different kinds of society rites he had mentioned, thanks to the generous hospitality of my friends in New York, I only knew the English functions from a very brief stay in England on my way here, and from what I had read of them in English fiction, and in the relations of our emissaries. He inquired into our emissary system, and the company appeared greatly interested in such account of it as I could briefly give.

"Well," he said, "that would do while you kept to yourselves; but now that your country is opened to the plutocratic world, your public documents will be apt to come back to the countries your emissaries have visited, and make trouble. The first thing you know some of our bright reporters will get onto one of your emissaries, and interview him, and then we shall get what you think of us at first hands. By the way, have you seen any of those primitive social delights which Mrs. Makely regrets so much?"

"I?" our hostess protested. But, then, she perceived that he was joking, and she let me answer.

I said that I had seen them nearly all, during the past year, in New England and in the West, but they appeared to me inalienably of the simpler life of the country, and that I was not surprised they should not have found an evolution in the more artificial society of the cities.

"I see," he returned, "that you reserve your *opinion* of our more artificial society; but you may be sure that our reporters will get it out of you yet, before you leave us."

"Those horrid reporters!" one of the ladies irrelevantly sighed.

The gentleman resumed: "In the meantime, I don't mind saying how it strikes me. I think you are quite right about the indigenous American things being adapted only to the simpler life of the country and the small towns. It is so everywhere. As soon as people become at all refined, they look down upon what is their own as something vulgar. But it is peculiarly so with us. We have nothing national that is not connected with the life of work, and when we begin to live the life of pleasure, we must borrow from the people abroad, who have always lived the life of pleasure."

"Mr. Homos, you know," Mrs. Makely explained for me, as if this were the aptest moment, "thinks we all ought to work. He thinks we oughtn't to have any servants."

"Oh, no, dear lady," I put in. "I don't think that of you, as you *are*. None of you could see more plainly than I do, that in your conditions you *must* have servants, and that you cannot possibly work, unless poverty obliges you."

The other ladies had turned upon me with surprise and horror at Mrs. Makely's words, but they now apparently relented, as if I had fully redeemed myself from the charge made against me. Mrs. Strange alone seemed to have found nothing monstrous in my supposed position. "Sometimes," she said, "I wish we had to work, all of us, and that we could be freed from our servile bondage to servants."

Several of the ladies admitted that it was the greatest slavery in the world, and that it would be comparative luxury to do one's own work. But they all asked, in one form or another, what were they to do, and Mrs. Strange owned that she did not know. The facetious gentleman asked me how the ladies did in Altruria, and when I told them, as well as I could, they were, of course, very civil about it, but I could see that they all thought it impossible, or, if not impossible, then ridiculous. I did not feel bound to defend our customs, and I knew very well that each woman there was imagining herself in our conditions with the curse of her plutocratic tradition still upon her. They could not do otherwise, any of them, and they seemed to get tired of such effort as they did make.

Mrs. Makely rose, and the other ladies rose with her, for the Americans follow the English custom in letting the men remain at table after the women have left. But on this occasion I found it varied, by a pretty touch from the French custom, and the men, instead of merely standing up while the women filed out, gave each his arm, as far as the drawing-room, to the lady he had brought in to dinner. Then we went back, and what is the pleasantest part of the dinner to most men began for us.

I must say, to the credit of the Americans, that although the eating and drinking among them appear gross enough to an Altrurian, you are not often revolted by the coarse stories which the English tell as soon as the ladies have left them. If it is a men's dinner, or more especially a men's supper, these stories are pretty sure to follow the coffee; but when there have been women at the board, some sense of their presence seems to linger in the more delicate American nerves, and the indulgence is limited to two or three things off color, as the phrase is here, told with anxious glances at the drawing-room doors, to see if they are fast shut.

I do not remember just what brought the talk back from these primrose paths, to that question of American society forms, but presently some one said he believed the church sociable was the thing in most towns beyond the apple-bee and sugar-party stage, and this opened the inquiry as to how far the church still formed the social life of the people in cities. Some one suggested that in Brooklyn it formed it altogether, and then they laughed, for Brooklyn is always a joke with the New Yorkers; I do not know exactly why, except that this vast city is so largely a suburb, and that it has a great number of churches, and is comparatively cheap. Then another told of a lady who had come to New York (he admitted, twenty years ago,) and was very lonely, as she had no letters, until she joined a church. This at once brought her a general acquaintance, and she began to find herself in society; but as soon as she did so, she joined a more exclusive church where they took no notice of strangers. They all laughed at that bit of human nature, as they called it, and they philosophized the relation of women to society as a purely business relation. The talk ranged to the mutable character of society, and how people got into it, and were of it, and how it was very different from what it once was, except that with women it was always business. They spoke of certain new rich people with affected contempt; but I could see that they were each proud of knowing such millionaires as they could claim for acquaintance, though they pretended to make fun of the number of men-servants you had to run the gauntlet of in their houses before you could get to your hostess.

One of my commensals said he had noticed that I took little or no wine, and when I said that we seldom drank it in Altruria, he answered that he did not think I could make that go in America, if I meant to dine much. "Dining, you know, means overeating," he explained, "and if you wish to overeat, you must overdrink. I venture to say that you will pass a worse night than any of us, Mr. Homos, and that you will be sorrier to-morrow than I shall." They were all smoking, and I confess that their tobacco was secretly such an affliction to me that I was at one moment in doubt whether I should take a cigar myself, or ask leave to join the ladies.

The gentleman who had talked so much already said: "Well, I don't mind dining so much, especially with Makely, here, but I do object to supping, as I have to do now and then, in the way of pleasure. Last Saturday night I sat down at eleven o'clock to blue-point oysters, consommé soup, stewed terrapin — yours was very good, Makely; I wish I had taken more of it — lamb chops with peas, redhead duck with celery mayonnaise, Nesselrode pudding, fruit, cheese, and coffee, with sausages, caviare, radishes, celery, and olives interspersed wildly, and drinkables and smokables ad libitum; and I can assure you that I felt very devout when I woke up after churchtime in the morning. It is this turning night into day that is killing us. We men, who have to go to business the next morning, ought to strike, and say we won't go to anything later than eight o'clock dinner."

"Ah, then the women would insist upon our making it four o'clock tea," said another.

Our host seemed to be reminded of something by the mention of the women, and he said, after a glance round at the state of the different cigars, "Shall we join the ladies?"

One of the men-servants had evidently been waiting for this question. He held the door open, and we all filed into the drawing-room.

Mrs. Makely hailed me with, "Ah, Mr. Homos, I'm so glad you've come! We poor women have been having the most dismal time!"

"Honestly," asked the funny gentleman, "don't you always, without us?"

"Yes, but this has been worse than usual. Mrs. Strange has been asking us how many people we supposed there were in this city, within five minutes' walk of us, who had no dinner to-day. Do you call that kind?"

"A little more than kin, and less than kind, perhaps," the gentleman suggested. "But what does she propose to do about it?"

He turned toward Mrs. Strange, who answered, "Nothing. What does any one propose to do about it?"

"Then, why do you think about it?"

"I don't. It thinks about itself. Do you know that poem of Longfellow's, 'The Challenge'?"

"No, I never heard of it."

"Well, it begins in his sweet old way, about some Spanish king, who was killed before a city he was besieging, and one of his knights sallies out of the camp, and challenges the people of the city, the living and the dead, as traitors. Then the poet breaks off, *apropos de rien:*

> 'There is a greater army
> That besets us round with strife,
> A numberless, starving army,
> At all the gates of life.
> The poverty-stricken millions
> Who challenge our wine and bread,
> And impeach us all for traitors,
> Both the living and the dead.
> And whenever I sit at the banquet,
> Where the feast and song are high,
> Amid the mirth and the music
> I can hear that fearful cry.
> And hollow and haggard faces
> Look into the lighted hall,
> And wasted hands are extended
> To catch the crumbs that fall.
> For within there is light and plenty,
> And odors fill the air;
> But without there is cold and darkness,
> And hunger and despair.
> And there, in the camp of famine,
> In wind and cold and rain,
> Christ, the great Lord of the Army,
> Lies dead upon the plain.'"

"Ah," said the facetious gentleman, "that is fine! We really forget how fine Longfellow was. It is so pleasant to hear you quoting poetry, Mrs. Strange. That sort of thing has almost gone out; and it's a pity."

A. HOMOS.

LETTERS OF AN ALTRURIAN TRAVELLER.

BY W. D. HOWELLS.

THE SELLING AND THE GIVING OF DINNERS.

IX.

New York, December 15, 1893.
My dear Cyril:

In answer to the inquiry in your last letter concerning the large shops here, I cannot say they are very attractive, and as I have told you, they are not so many as we have been led to suppose. There are, perhaps, fifty, at most, on Broadway and the different avenues. They are vast emporiums, sometimes occupying half a city-block, and multiplying their acreage of floor space by repeated stories, one above another, reached by elevators perpetually lifting and lowering the throngs of shoppers. But I do not find any principle of taste governing the arrangement of their multitudinous wares; and they have always a huddled and confused effect. I miss the precious and human quality of individuality in them. I meet no one who seems to have a personal interest in the goods or the customers; it is a dry and cold exchange of moneys and wares; and the process is made the more tedious by the checks used to keep the salesmen and saleswomen from robbing their employers. They take your money, but it must be sent with their written account and your purchase to a central bureau, where the account is audited and returned with your purchase, after a vexatious delay. But in the system of things here, fully a fifth of the people seem employed in watching that the rest do not steal, and fully a fifth of the time is lost.

You have perhaps imagined these great stores like our Regionic bazaars, where we go with our government orders to supply our needs, or indulge our fancies. But they are not at all like these, except in their vastness and variety. I cannot say that there is no aim at beauty in their display, but the sordid motive of advertising running through it all destroys this. You are not pressed to buy, here, any more than with us, and the salespeople are not allowed to misrepresent the quality of the goods, for that would be bad business; but the affair is a purely business transaction. That friendly hospitality which our bazaars show all comers, and that cordial endeavor to seek out and satisfy their desires are wholly unknown here. What you experience is the working of a vast, very intricate, and rather clumsy money-making machine, with yourself as a part of the mechanism.

For this reason I prefer the smaller shops where I can enter into some human relation with the merchant, if it is only for the moment. I have already tried to give you some notion of the multitude of these; and I must say now that they add much in their infinite number and variety to such effect of gaiety as the city has. They are especially attractive at night, where, under favor of the prevailing dark, the shapeless monster is able to hide something of its deformity. Then the brilliant lamps, with the shadows they cast, unite to an effect of gaiety which the day will not allow.

The great stores contribute nothing to this, however, for they all close at six o'clock in the evening. On the other hand, they do not mar such poor beauty as the place has with the multitude of signs that the minor traffic renders itself so offensive with. One sign, rather simple and unostentatious, suffices for a large store; a little store will want half a dozen, and will have them painted and hung all over its façade, and stood about in front of it as obtrusively as the police will permit. The effect is bizarre and grotesque beyond expression. If one thing in the business streets makes New York more hideous than another it is the signs, with their discordant colors, their infinite variety of tasteless shapes. If by chance there is any architectural beauty in a business edifice, it is spoiled, insulted, outraged by these huckstering appeals; while the prevailing unsightliness is emphasized and heightened by them. A vast, hulking, bare brick wall, rising six or seven stories above the neighboring buildings, you would think bad enough in all conscience: how, then, shall I give you any notion of the horror it becomes when its unlovely space is blocked out in a ground of white with a sign painted on it in black letters ten feet high?

But you could not imagine the least offensive of the signs that deface American cities, where they seem trying to shout and shriek each other down, wherever one turns; they cover the fronts and sides and tops of the edifices; they deface the rocks of the meadows and the cliffs of the rivers; they stretch on long extents of fencing in the vacant suburban lands, and cover the roofs and sides of the barns. The darkness does not shield you from them, and by night the very sky is starred with the electric bulbs that spell out, on the roofs of the lofty city edifices, the frantic announcement of this or that business enterprise.

The strangest part of all this is, no one finds it offensive, or at least no one says that it is offensive. It is, indeed, a necessary phase of the economic warfare in which this people live, for the most as unconsciously as people lived in feudal cities, while the nobles fought out their private quarrels in the midst of them. No one dares relax his vigilance or his activity in the commercial strife, and in the absence of any public opinion, or any public sentiment concerning them, it seems as if the signs might eventually hide the city. That would not be so bad if something could then be done to hide the signs.

Nothing seems so characteristic of this city, after its architectural shapelessness, as the eating and drinking constantly going on in it. I do not mean, now, the eating and drinking in society alone, though from the fact that some sort of repast is made the occasion of nearly every social meeting, you might well suppose that society was altogether devoted to eating and drinking, and that this phase of the feasting might altogether occupy one. But I was thinking of the restaurants and hotels, of every kind and quality, and the innumerable saloons and bars. There may not be really more of them in New York, in proportion to the population than in other great plutocratic cities, but there are apparently more; for in this, as in all her other characteristics, New York is very open; her virtues and her vices, her luxury and her misery, are in plain sight, so that no one can fail of them; and I fancy that a famishing man must suffer peculiarly here from the spectacle of people everywhere visible at sumptuous tables.

Many of the finest hotels, if not most of them, have their dining-rooms on the level of the street, and the windows, whether curtained or uncurtained, reveal the continual riot within. I confess that the effect upon some hungry passer is always so present to my imagination that I shun the places near the windows; but the Americans are so used to the perpetual encounter of famine and of surfeit in their civilization, that they do not seem to mind it; and one of them very logically made me observe when he conceived my reluctance, that I was not relieving anybody's want when I chose an uncomfortable place on the dark side of the room. It was, indeed, an instance of the unavailing self-denial so frequent here. Still, I prefer either the restaurants in the basements or on the second floor; and these are without number, too, though I do not think they are so many as the others; at least they do not make as much effect. But of every sort, as I say, there is an immense variety, because New York is so largely a city of strangers, whose pleasures or affairs call them here by whole populations. Every day the trains and boats fetch and carry hundreds of thousands of visitors, who must be somehow housed and fed, and who find shelter in the hotels, and food wherever they happen to be at the moment of lunch or dinner.

But the restaurants have to cater besides to the far vaster custom of the business men who live at such a distance from their shops and offices that they never take the midday meal with their families except on Sunday. So far they are like the workingmen, whom you see seated on piles of rubbish in the street, with their dinner-pails between their knees; but I need not tell you that the business men are not so simple or so sparing in the satisfaction of their hunger. I am not sure that they are always much more comfortable; and in fine weather I think I would rather sit out doors on a heap of brick or lumber than on a bracketed stool-top before a lunch-counter amidst a turmoil of crockery and cookery that I should in vain try to give you a sense of. These lunch-counters abound everywhere, and thousands throng them every day, snatching the meat and drink pushed across the counter to them by the waiters from the semi-circle within, and then making room for others. But of late, a new kind of lunch-room has come into fashion, which I wish you could see, both for the sake of the curious spectacle it affords, and the philosophy it involves. You would find yourself in a long room, if you came with me, where you would see rows of large chairs, each with one arm made wide enough to hold a cup and saucer, and a plate. At a convenient place in the room is a counter or table, with cups for tea and coffee set out on it, and plates of pie, sandwiches, and such viands as need not be cut with a knife, and may be gathered up in the fingers. Each comer goes up to the counter, and takes from it what he likes and carries it off to some chair, where he eats his lunch in peace, and then goes back to the counter and pays for it. His word is implicitly taken as to what he has had; he goes as he came, without question; and the host finds his account in the transaction; for even if he is now and then cheated, he saves the cost of a troop of waiters by letting his guests serve themselves, and he is able for the same reason to afford his provisions at half the price they must pay elsewhere. His experience is that he is almost never cheated, and the Altrurian theory of human nature, that if you will use men fairly and trust them courageously, they will not betray you, finds practical endorsement in it.

Most of the better class of clerks and small business men frequent the chop-houses, which affect the back rooms of old-fashioned dwellings, and the basement restaurants in the cellarways of business buildings, down town. Some of the lofty edifices which deform that quarter of the city have restaurants in them on a grand scale, as to prices and fare, and all the appointments of the table; these are for a still better sort of lunchers, or richer sort (you always say better when you mean richer, in America), and these often have lunch clubs, of difficult membership, and with rooms luxuriously appointed, where, if they choose, people can linger over their claret and cigars as quietly as if they were in their own houses. Sometimes a whole house is fitted up with all the comforts of a club, which is frequented by its members, or the greater part of them, only for luncheon. Others, of the kind which form effectively the home of their members, are resorted to at midday by all who do business within easy reach of them; though the breakfasting and dining goes on there, too, day in and day out, as constantly as at private houses. In fact, the chief use of the clubs is through their excellent kitchens.

There are foreign restaurants in all parts of the town,—French, German, Italian, Spanish,—where you can have your lunch served in courses at a fixed sum for the whole. The Hebrews, who are so large and so prosperous an element of the commercial body of New York, have restaurants of this sort, where they incur no peril of pork, or meat of any kind that is not *kosher*. Signs in Hebrew give them warrant of the fact that nothing unclean, or that has been rendered unlawful by hanging from a nail, is served within; and the Christian, if he sits down at a table, is warned that he can have neither milk nor butter with his meat, since this is against their ancient and most wholesome law.

Far round on the East side, and in all the poorer quarters of the town, there are eating-houses and cook-shops of lower and lower grade, which are resorted to by those workingmen who do not bring their dinners with them in pails, or who would rather take their drink and their food together. But these are seldom the older-fashioned laborers, of Irish or American descent; the frequenters of such places are Germans or Italians, or of the newer immigrations from eastern Europe, who find there some suggestions of their national dishes, and some touch of art in the cookery, no matter how common and vile the material. This, as you see it in the butcher-shops and the greengrocers of those parts, is often revolting and unwholesome enough — pieces of loathsome carnage, and bits of decaying vegetation. It is to be supposed that the poorer restaurants supply themselves from the superfluity of the better sort and of the hotels, but this is not always the case. In many cases, the hotels cast this into the great heap of offal, which the garbage carts of the city dump into the vessels used to carry it out to sea, so that not even the swine may eat of it, much less the thousands of hungering men and women and children, who never know what it is to have quite enough. But this is only one phase of the wilful waste that in manifold ways makes such woeful want in plutocratic conditions. Every comfortable family in this city throws away at every meal the sustenance of some other family; or, if not that then, so much at least as would keep it from starvation. The predatory instinct is very subtle, and people who live upon each other, instead of for each other, have shrewdly contrived profit within profit until it is hard to say whether many things you consume have any value in themselves at all. If they could be brought at once to the consumer they would cost infinitely little, almost nothing; but they reach him only after half a dozen sterile agencies have had their usury of them; and then they are most wonderfully, most wickedly wasted in the system of each household having its own black, noisy, unwholesome kitchen, with a cook in it chiefly skilled to spoil God's gifts.

From time to time, there is great talk in the newspapers of abolishing the middlemen, as the successive hucksters are called; but there is no way of doing this, short of abolishing the whole plutocratic system, for the middleman is the business man, and the business man is the cornerstone of this civilization; if, indeed, a civilization which seems poised in air by studying the trick of holding itself from the ground by the waistband, can be said to have any foundation whatever.

There is not so much hope of the middleman's going as there is of the individual kitchen's, which really seems threatened, at times, by the different new ways of living which Mrs. Makely, you remember, told me of. It is, in fact, a survival of the simpler time when the housewife prepared the food of her family herself; but that time is long past, with the well-to-do Americans, and what was once the focal center of the home, has no longer any just place in it, and only forms the great rent through which half the husband's earnings escape. Yet, if I tell them of our coöperative housekeeping, they make the answer which they seem to think serves all occasions, and say that such a system will do very well for Altruria, but that it is contrary to human nature, and it can never be made to work in America. They much prefer to go on wasting into the kitchen, and wasting out of it; the housewife either absolutely neglects her duty, or else she maddens herself with the care of it, and harries the poor drudge who slaves her life away in its heat and glare, and fails, with all her toil, of results which we have for a tithe of the cost and suffering.

But whenever I touch one of the points of economic contrast with ourselves, I feel as if I were giving it undue importance, for I think at once of a hundred others which seem to prove as conclusively that, as yet, the life of the Americans, in what most nearly concerns them, is not reasoned. They are where they are because some one else had arrived there before them, and they do most of the things that they do because the English do something like them. In a wholly different climate, a climate which touches both arctic and tropic extremes, they go on living as their ancestors lived in the equable seasons of the British Isles. They have not yet philosophized their food, or dress, or shelter, for their blazing summers, and swelter through them with such means of comfort as the ignorant usage of the mother-country provides.

In fact, the Americans have completed their reductio ad absurdum in pleasure as well as in business. Eating and drinking no longer suffice to bring people together, and the ladies say that if you want any one to come now, you must have something special to entertain your guests. You must have somebody sing, or recite, or play; I believe it has not yet come to a demand for hired dancing, as it presently will, if it does in London. Only very primitive people would now think of giving an afternoon tea without some special feature, though the at-homes still flourish, as a means of paying off the debts ladies owe one another for visits. Luncheons and dinners are given with a frequency that would imply the greatest financial prosperity, and the gayest social feeling as well as unlimited leisure, and unbounded hospitality. But these must always have some raison d'être, such as we do not dream of offering, who in our simplicity think it reason enough to ask our friends to join us at meat if we wish for their company. Here, apparently, no one wishes for your company personally, the individual is as completely lost in the social as he is in the economic scheme. You are invited as a factor in the problem which your hostess wishes to work out, and you are invited many days in advance, and sometimes several weeks; for every one is supposed to be in great request, and it is thought to be a sort of slight to bid a guest for any entertainment under a week, so that people excuse themselves for doing it.

Our fashion of offering hospitality on the impulse, would be as strange here as offering it without some special inducement for its acceptance. The inducement is, as often as can be, a celebrity or eccentricity of some sort, or some visiting foreigner; and I suppose that I have been a good deal used myself in one quality or the other. But when the thing has been done, fully and guardedly at all points, it does not seem to have been done for pleasure, either by the host or the guest. The dinner is given in payment of another dinner; or out of ambition by people who are striving to get forward in society; or by great social figures who give regularly a certain number of dinners every season. In either case it is eaten from motives at once as impersonal and as selfish. I do not mean to say that I have not been at many dinners where I felt nothing perfunctory either in host or guest, and where as sweet and gay a spirit ruled as at any of our own simple feasts. Still, I think your main impression of American hospitality would be that it was thoroughly infused with the plutocratic principle, and that it meant business.

I am speaking now of the hospitality of society people, who number, after all, but a few thousands out of the many millions of American people. These millions are so far from being in society, even when they are very comfortable, and on the way to great prosperity, if they are not already greatly prosperous, that if they were suddenly confronted with the best society of the great eastern cities they would find it almost as strange as so many Altrurians. A great part of them have no conception of entertaining except upon an Altrurian scale of simplicity, and they know nothing and care less for the forms that society people value themselves upon. Where they begin in the ascent of the social scale to adopt forms, it is still to wear them lightly and with an individual freedom and indifference; it is long before anxiety concerning the social law renders them vulgar.

Yet from highest to lowest, from first to last, one invariable fact characterizes them all, and it may be laid down as an axiom that in a plutocracy the man who needs a dinner, is the man who is never asked to dine. I do not say that he is not given a dinner. He is very often given a dinner, and for the most part he is kept from starving to death; but he is not suffered to sit at meat with his host, if the person who gives him a meal can be called his host. His need of the meal stamps him with a hopeless inferiority, and relegates him morally to the company of the swine at their husks, and of Lazarus whose sores the dogs licked. Usually, of course, he is not physically of such a presence as to fit him for any place in good society short of Abraham's bosom; but even if he were entirely decent, or of an inoffensive shabbiness, it would not be possible for his benefactor, in any grade of society, to ask him to his table. He is sometimes fed in the kitchen; where the people of the house feed in the kitchen themselves, he is fed at the back door.

We were talking of this the other night at the house of that lady whom Mrs. Makely invited me specially to meet on Thanksgiving Day. It happened then, as it often happens here, that although I was asked to meet her, I saw very little of her. It was not so bad as it sometimes is, for I have been asked to meet people, very informally, and passed the whole evening with them, and yet not exchanged a word with them. Mrs. Makely really gave me a seat next Mrs. Strange at table, and we had some unimportant conversation; but there was a lively little creature vis-à-vis of me, who had a fancy of addressing me so much of her talk, that my acquaintance with Mrs. Strange rather languished through the dinner, and she went away so soon after the men rejoined the ladies in the drawing-room, that I did not speak to her there. I was rather surprised, then, to receive a note from her a few days later, asking me to dinner ; and I finally went, I am ashamed to own, more from curiosity than from any other motive. I had been, in the meantime, thoroughly coached concerning her, by Mrs. Makely, whom I told of my invitation, and who said, quite frankly, that she wished Mrs. Strange had asked her, too. "But Eveleth Strange wouldn't do that," she explained, "because it would have the effect of paying me back. I'm so glad, on your account, that you're going, for I do want you to know at least one American woman that you can unreservedly approve of; I know you don't *begin* to approve of *me;* and I was so vexed that you really had no chance to talk with her that night you met her here; it seemed to me as if she ran away early, just to provoke me; and, to tell you the truth, I thought she had taken a dislike to you. I wish I could tell you just what sort of a person she is, but it would be perfectly hopeless, for you haven't got the documents, and you never could get them. I used to be at school with her, and even then she wasn't like any of the other girls. She was always so original, and did things from such a high motive, that afterwards, when we were all settled, I was perfectly thunderstruck at her marrying old Bellington Strange, who was twice her age, and had nothing but his money; he was not related to the New York Bellingtons at all, and nobody knows how he got the name; nobody ever heard of the Stranges. In fact, people said that he used to be plain Peter B. Strange, till he married Eveleth, and she made him drop the Peter, and blossom out in the Bellington, so that he could seem to have a social as well as a financial history. People who disliked her insisted that they were not in the least surprised at her marrying him; that the high-motive business was just her pose; and that she had simply got sick of being a teacher in a girls' school, and had jumped at the chance of getting him. But I always stuck up for her,—and I know that she did it for the sake of her family, who were all as poor as poor, and were dependent on her after her father went to smash in his business. She was always as high-strung and as romantic as she could be, but I don't believe that even then she would have taken Mr. Strange, if there had been anybody else. I don't suppose any one else ever looked at her, for the young men are pretty sharp nowadays, and are not going to marry girls without a cent, when there are so many rich girls, just as charming every way : you can't expect them to. At any rate, whatever her motive was, she had her reward, for Mr. Strange died within a year of their marriage, and she got all his money. There was no attempt to break the will, for Mr. Strange seemed to be literally of no family; and she's lived quietly on in the house he bought her, ever since, except when she's in Europe, and that's about two-thirds of the time. She has her mother with her, and I suppose that her sisters, and her cousins, and her aunts, come in for outdoor aid. She's always helping somebody. They say that's her pose, now; but if it is, I don't think it's a bad one; and certainly if she wanted to get married again, there would be no trouble, with her three millions. I advise you to go to her dinner, by all means, Mr. Homos. It will be something worth while, in every way, and perhaps you'll convert her to Altrurianism; she's as hopeful a subject as *I* know."

I was one of the earliest of her guests, for I cannot yet believe that people do not want me to come exactly when they say they do. I perceived, however, that one other gentleman had come before me, and I was both surprised and delighted to find that this was my acquaintance, Mr. Bullion, the Boston banker. He professed as much pleasure at our meeting as I certainly felt; but after a few words he went on talking with Mrs. Strange, while I was left to her mother, an elderly woman of quiet and even timid bearing, who affected me at once as born and bred in a wholly different environment. In fact, every American of the former generation is almost as strange to it in tradition, though not in principle, as I am; and I found myself singularly at home with this sweet lady, who seemed glad of my interest in her. I was taken from her side to be introduced to a lady, on the opposite side of the room, who said she had been promised my acquaintance by a friend of hers, whom I had met in the mountains,—Mr. Twelvemough; did I remember him? She gave a little cry while still speaking, and dramatically stretched her hand toward a gentleman who entered at the moment, and whom I saw to be no other than Mr. Twelvemough himself. As soon as he had greeted our hostess he hastened up to us, and barely giving himself time to press the still outstretched hand of my companion, shook mine warmly, and expressed the greatest joy at seeing me. He said that he had just got back to town, in a manner, and had not known I was here, till Mrs. Strange had asked him to meet me. There were not a great many other guests, when they all arrived, and we sat down, a party not much larger than at Mrs. Makely's.

I found that I was again to take out my hostess, but I was put next the lady with whom I had been talking; she had come without her husband, who was, apparently, of a different social taste from herself, and had an engagement of his own; there was an artist and his wife whose looks I liked; some others whom I need not specify, were there, I fancied, because they had heard of Altruria, and were curious to see me. As Mr. Twelvemough sat quite at the other end of the table, the lady on my right could easily ask me whether I liked his books. She said, tentatively, people liked them because they felt sure when they took up one of his novels they had not got hold of a tract on political economy in disguise.

It was this complimentary close of a remark which scarcely began with praise, that made itself heard across the table, and was echoed with a heartfelt sigh from the lips of another lady.

"Yes," she said, "that is what I find such a comfort in Mr. Twelvemough's books."

"We were *speaking* of Mr. Twelvemough's books," triumphed the first lady, and then several began to extol them for being fiction pure and simple, and not dealing with any question but the loves of young people.

Mr. Twelvemough sat looking as modest as he could under the praise, and one of the ladies said that in a novel she had lately read there was a description of a surgical operation, that made her feel as if she had been present at a clinic. Then the author said that he had read that passage, too, and found it extremely well done. It was fascinating, but it was not art.

The painter asked, "Why was it not art?"

The author answered, "Well, if such a thing as that was art, then anything that a man chose to do in a work of imagination was art."

"Precisely," said the painter, "art *is* choice."

"On that ground," the banker interposed, "you could say that political economy was a fit subject for art, if an artist chose to treat it."

"It would have its difficulties," the painter admitted, "but there are certain phases of political economy, dramatic moments, human moments, which might be very fitly treated in art. For instance, who would object to Mr. Twelvemough's describing an eviction from an East side tenement-house on a cold winter night, with the mother and her children huddled about the fire the father had kindled with pieces of the household furniture?"

"*I* should object very much, for one," said the lady who had objected to the account of the surgical operation. "It would be too creepy. Art should give pleasure."

"Then you think a tragedy is not art?" asked the painter.

"I think that these harrowing subjects are brought in altogether too much," said the lady. "There are enough of them in real life, without filling all the novels with them. It's terrible the number of beggars you meet on the street, this winter. Do you want to meet them in Mr. Twelvemough's novels, too?"

"Well, it wouldn't cost me any money, there. I shouldn't have to give."

"You oughtn't to give money in real life," said the lady. "You ought to give charity tickets. If the beggars refuse them, it shows they are imposters."

"It's some comfort to know that the charities are so active," said the elderly young lady, "even if half the letters one gets *do* turn out to be appeals from them."

"It's very disappointing to have them do it, though," said the artist, lightly. "I thought there was a society to abolish poverty. That doesn't seem to be so active as the charities this winter. Is it possible they've found it a failure?"

"Well," said Mr. Bullion, "perhaps they have suspended during the hard times."

They tossed the ball back and forth with a lightness the Americans have, and I could not have believed, if I had not known how hardened people become to such things here, that they were almost in the actual presence of hunger and cold. It was within five minutes' walk of their warmth and surfeit; and if they had lifted the window and called, "Who goes there?" the houselessness that prowls the night, could have answered them from the street below, "Despair!"

"I had an amusing experience," Mr. Twelvemough began, "when I was doing a little visiting for the charities in our ward, the other winter."

"For the sake of the literary material?" suggested the artist.

"Partly for the sake of the literary material; you know we have to look for our own everywhere. But we had a case of an old actor's son, who had got out of all the places he had filled, on account of rheumatism, and could not go to sea, or drive a truck, or even wrap gas-fixtures in paper any more."

"A checkered employ," the banker mused aloud.

"It was not of a simultaneous nature," the novelist explained. "So he came on the charities, and as I knew the theatrical profession a little, and how generous it was with all related to it, I said that I would undertake to look after his case. You know the theory is that we get work for our patients, or clients, or whatever they are, and I went to a manager whom I knew to be a good fellow, and I asked him for some sort of work. He said, Yes, send the man round, and he would give him a job copying parts for a new play he had written."

The novelist paused, and nobody laughed.

"It seems to me that your experience is instructive, rather than amusing," said the banker. "It shows that something can be done, if you try."

"Well," said Mr. Twelvemough, "I thought that was the moral, myself, till the fellow came afterwards to thank me. He said that he considered himself very lucky, for the manager had told him that there were six other men had wanted that job."

Everybody laughed, now, and I looked at my hostess in a little bewilderment. She murmured, "I suppose the joke is that he had befriended one man at the expense of six others."

"Oh," I returned, "is that a joke?"

No one answered, but the lady at my right asked: "How do you manage with poverty in Altruria?"

I saw the banker fix a laughing eye on me, but I answered, "In Altruria we have no poverty."

"Ah, I knew you would say that!" he cried out. "That's what he always does," he explained to the lady. "Bring up any one of our little difficulties, and ask how they get over it in Altruria, and he says they have nothing like it. It's very simple."

They all began to ask me questions, but with a courteous incredulity, which I could feel well enough, and some of my answers made them laugh, all but my hostess, who received them with a gravity that finally prevailed. But I was not disposed to go on talking of Altruria then, though they all protested a real interest, and murmured against the hardship of being cut off with so brief an account of our country as I had given them.

"Well," said the banker at last, "if there is no cure for our poverty, we might as well go on and enjoy ourselves."

"Yes," said our hostess, with a sad little smile, "we might as well enjoy ourselves."

A. HOMOS.

[*To be concluded in the September issue.*]

LETTERS OF AN ALTRURIAN TRAVELLER.

By W. D. Howells.

AN ALTRUISTIC PLUTOCRAT.

X.

New York, December 16, 1893.
My dear Cyril:

The talk at Mrs. Strange's table took a far wider range than my meager notes would intimate, and we sat so long that it was almost eleven before the men joined the ladies in the drawing-room. You will hardly conceive of remaining two, three, or four hours at dinner, as one often does here, in society. Out of society, the meals are dispatched with a rapidity unknown to the Altrurians. Our habit of listening to the lectors, especially at the evening repast, and then of reasoning upon what we have heard, prolongs our stay at the board; but the fondest listener, the greatest talker among us, would be impatient of the delay eked out here by the great number, and the slow procession of the courses served. Yet the poorest American would find his ideal realized rather in the long-drawn-out gluttony of the society dinner here, than in our temperate simplicity.

At such a dinner it is very hard to avoid a surfeit, and I have to guard myself very carefully, lest, in the excitement of the talk, I gorge myself with everything, in its turn. Even at the best, my overloaded stomach often joins with my conscience in reproaching me for what you would think a shameful excess at table. Yet, wicked as my riot is, my waste is worse, and I have to think with contrition, not only of what I have eaten, but of what I have left uneaten, in a city where so many wake and sleep in hunger.

The ladies made a show of lingering, after we joined them in the drawing-room; but there were furtive glances at the clock, and presently her guests began to bid Mrs. Strange good-night. When I came up, and offered her my hand, she would not take it, but murmured, with a kind of passion: "Don't go! I mean it! Stay, and tell us about Altruria,—my mother and me!"

I was by no means loth, for I must confess that all I had seen and heard of this lady interested me in her more and more. I felt at home with her, too, as with no other society woman I have met; she seemed to me not only good, but very sincere, and very good-hearted, in spite of the world she lived in. Yet I have met so many disappointments here, of the kind that our civilization wholly fails to prepare us for, that I should not have been surprised to find that Mrs. Strange had wished me to stay, not that she might hear me talk about Altruria, but that I might hear her talk about herself. You must understand that the essential vice of a system which concenters a human being's thoughts upon his own interests, from the first moment of responsibility, colors and qualifies every motive with egotism. All egotists are unconscious, for otherwise they would be intolerable to themselves; but some are subtler than others; and as most women have finer natures than most men, everywhere, and in America most women have finer minds than most men, their egotism usually takes the form of pose. This is often obvious, but in some cases it is so delicately managed that you do not suspect it, unless some other woman gives you a hint of it, and even then you cannot be sure of it, seeing the self-sacrifice, almost to martyrdom, which the poseuse makes for it. If Mrs. Makely had not suggested that some people attributed a pose to Mrs. Strange, I should certainly never have dreamed of looking for it, and I should have been only intensely interested, when she began, as soon as I was left alone with her and her mother:

"You may not know how unusual I am in asking this favor of you, Mr. Homos; but you might as well learn from me as from others, that I am rather unusual in everything. In fact, you can report in Altruria, when you get home, that you found at least one woman in America, whom fortune had smiled upon in every way, and who hated her smiling fortune almost as much as she hated herself. I'm quite satisfied," she went on, with a sad mockery, "that fortune is a man, and an American; when he has given you all the materials for having a good time, he believes that you must be happy, because there is nothing to hinder. It isn't that I want to be happy in the greedy way that men think we do, for then I could easily be happy. If you have a soul which is not above buttons, buttons are enough. But if you expect to be of real use, to help on, and to help out, you will be disappointed. I have not the faith that they say upholds you Altrurians in trying to help out, if I didn't see my way out. It seems to me that my reason has some right to satisfaction, and that, if I am a woman grown, I can't be satisfied with the assurances they would give to little girls, that everything is going on well. Any one can see that things are not going on well. There is more and more wretchedness of every kind, not hunger of body alone, but hunger of soul. If you escape one, you suffer the other, because, if you *have* a soul, you must long to help, not for a time, but for all time. I suppose," she asked, abruptly, "that Mrs. Makely has told you something about me?"

"Something," I admitted.

"I ask," she went on, "because I don't want to bore you with a statement of my case, if you know it already. Ever since I heard you were in New York, I have wished to see you, and to talk with you about Altruria; I did not suppose that there would be any chance at Mrs. Makely's, and there wasn't; and I did not suppose there would be any chance here, unless I could take courage to do what I have done, now. You must excuse it, if it seems as extraordinary a proceeding to you as it really is; I wouldn't at all have you think it is usual for a lady to ask one of her guests to stay after the rest, in order, if you please, to confess herself to him. It's a crime without a name."

She laughed, not gaily, but humorously, and then went on, speaking always with a feverish eagerness, which I find it hard to give you a sense of, for the women here have an intensity quite beyond our experience of the sex at home:

"But you are a foreigner, and you come from an order of things so utterly unlike ours, that perhaps you will be able to condone my offense. At any rate, I have risked it." She laughed again, more gaily, and recovered herself in a cheerfuller and easier mood. "Well, the long and the short of it is, that I have come to the end of my tether. I have tried, as truly as I believe any woman ever did, to do my share, with money and with work, to help make life better for those whose life is bad, and though one mustn't boast of good works, I may say that I have been pretty thorough, and if I've given up, it's because I see, in our state of things, *no* hope of curing the evil. It's like trying to soak up the drops of a rainstorm. You do dry a drop here and there; but the clouds are full of them, and the first thing you know, you stand, with your blotting-paper in your hand, in a puddle over your shoe-top. There is nothing but charity, and charity is a failure, except for the moment. If you think of the misery around you, and that must remain around you, forever and ever, as long as you live, you have your choice—to go mad, and be put into an asylum, or go mad, and devote yourself to society."

While Mrs. Strange talked on, her mother listened quietly, with a dim, submissive smile, and her hands placidly crossed in her lap. She now said:

"It seems to be very different now from what it was in my time. There are certainly a great many beggars, and we used never to have one. Children grew up, and people lived and died, in large towns, without ever seeing one. I remember, when my husband first took me abroad, how astonished we were at the beggars. Now, I meet as many in New York, as I met in London, or in Rome. But if you don't do charity, what can you do? Christ enjoined it, and Paul said—"

"Oh, people *never* do the charity that Christ meant," said Mrs. Strange; "and, as things are now, how *could* they? Who would dream of dividing half her frocks and wraps with poor women, or selling *all*, and giving to the poor? That is what makes it so hopeless. We *know* that Christ was perfectly right, and that he was perfectly sincere in what he said to the good young millionaire; but we all go away exceeding sorrowful, just as the good young millionaire did. We have to, if we don't want to come on charity ourselves. How do *you* manage about that?" she asked me; and then she added, "But, of course, I forgot that you have no need of charity."

"Oh, yes, we have," I returned; and I tried, once more, as I have tried so often with Americans, to explain how the heavenly need of giving the self continues with us, but on terms that do not harrow the conscience of the giver, as self-sacrifice always must here, at its purest and noblest. I sought to make her conceive of our nation as a family, where every one was secured against want by the common provision, and against the degrading and depraving inequality which comes from want. The "dead-level of equality" is what the Americans call the condition in which all would be as the angels of God, and they blasphemously deny that He ever meant His creatures to be alike happy, because some, through a long succession of unfair advantages, have inherited more brain, or brawn, or beauty, than others. I found that this gross and impious notion of God darkened even the clear intelligence of a woman like Mrs. Strange; and, indeed, it prevails here so commonly, that it is one of the first things advanced as an argument against the Altrurianization of America.

I believe I did, at last, succeed in showing her how charity still continues among us, but in forms that bring neither a sense of inferiority to him who takes, nor anxiety to him who gives. I said that benevolence here often seemed to involve, essentially, some such risk as a man should run if he parted with a portion of the vital air which belonged to himself and his family, in succoring a fellow-being from suffocation; but that with us, where it was no more possible for one to deprive himself of his share of the common food, shelter, and clothing, than of the air he breathed, one could devote one's self utterly to others, without that foul alloy of fear, which I thought must basely qualify every good deed in plutocratic conditions.

She said that she knew what I meant, and that I was quite right in my conjecture, as regarded men, at least; a man who did not stop to think what the effect, upon himself and his own, his giving must have, would be a fool or a madman; but women could often give as recklessly as they spent, without any thought of consequences, for they did not know how money came.

"Women," I said, "are exterior to your conditions, and they can sacrifice themselves without wronging any one."

"Or, rather," she continued, "without the sense of wronging any one. Our men like to keep us in that innocence, or ignorance; they think it is pretty, or they think it is funny; and as long as a girl is in her father's house, or a wife is in her husband's, she knows no more of money-earning, or money-making, than a child. Most grown women, among us, if they had a sum of money in the bank, would not know how to get it out. They would not know how to endorse a check, much less draw one. But there are plenty of women who are inside the conditions, as much as men are: poor women who have to earn their bread, and rich women who have to manage their property. I can't speak for the poor women; but I can speak for the rich, and I can confess for them that what you imagine is true. The taint of unfaith and distrust is on every dollar that you dole out, so that, as far as the charity of the rich is concerned, I would read Shakespeare:

"It curseth him that gives, and him that takes."

"Perhaps that is why the rich give comparatively so little! The poor can never understand how much the rich value their money, how much the owner of a great fortune dreads to see it less! If it were not so, they would surely give more than they do; for a man who has ten millions could give eight of them, without feeling the loss; the man with a hundred could give ninety, and be no nearer want. Ah, it's a strange mystery! My poor husband and I used to talk of it a great deal, in the long year that he lay dying; and I think I hate my superfluity the more because I know he hated it so much."

A little trouble had stolen into her impassioned tones, and there was a gleam, as of tears, in the eyes she dropped for a moment. They were shining still, when she lifted them again to mine.

"I suppose," she said, "that Mrs. Makely told you something of my marriage?"

"Eveleth!" her mother protested, with a gentle murmur.

"Oh, I think I can be frank with Mr. Homos! He is not an American, and he will understand, or, at least, he will not misunderstand. Besides, I dare say I shall not say anything worse than Mrs. Makely has said already! My husband was much older than I, and I ought not to have married him; a young girl ought never to marry an old man, or even a man who is only a good many years her senior. But we both faithfully tried to make the best of our mistake, not the worst, and I think this effort helped us to respect each other, when there couldn't be any question of more. He was a rich man, and he had made his money out of nothing, or, at least, from a beginning of utter poverty. But in his last years he came to a sense of its worthlessness, such as few men who have made their money ever have. He was a common man, in a great many ways; he was imperfectly educated, and he was ungrammatical, and he never was at home in society; but he had a tender heart, and an honest nature, and I revere his memory, as no one would believe I could without knowing him as I did. His money became a burden and a terror to him; he did not know what to do with it, and he was always morbidly afraid of doing harm with it; he got to thinking that money was an evil in itself."

"That is what we think," I ventured.

"Yes, I know. But he had thought this out for himself, and yet he had times when his thinking about it seemed to him a kind of craze, and, at any rate, he distrusted himself so much that he died leaving it all to me. I suppose he thought that, perhaps, I could learn how to give it without hurting; and then he knew that, in our state of things, I must have some money to keep the wolf from the door. And I am afraid to part with it, too. I have given, and given; but there seems some evil spell on the principal, that guards it from encroachment, so that it remains the same, and, if I do not watch, the interest grows in the bank, with that frightful life dead money seems endowed with, as the hair of dead people grows in the grave."

"Eveleth!" her mother murmured again.

"Oh, yes," she answered, "I dare say my words are wild. I dare say they only mean that I loathe my luxury from the bottom of my soul, and long to be rid of it, if I only could, without harm to others, and with safety to myself."

It seemed to me that I became suddenly sensible to this luxury for the first time. I had certainly been aware that I was in a large and stately house, and that I had been served and banquetted with a princely pride and profusion. But there had, somehow, been through all a sort of simplicity, a sort of retrusive quiet, so that I had not thought of the establishment, and its operation, even so much as I had thought of Mrs. Makely's far inferior scale of living; or, else, what with my going about so much in society, I was ceasing to be so keenly observant of the material facts as I had been at first. But I was better qualified to judge of what I saw, and I had now a vivid sense of the costliness of Mrs. Strange's environment. There were thousands of dollars in the carpets underfoot; there were tens of thousands in the pictures on the walls. In a bronze group that withdrew itself into a certain niche, with a faint relucence, there was the value of a skilled artisan's wage for five years of hard work; in the bindings of the books that showed from the library shelves, there was almost as much money as most of the authors had got for writing them. Every fixture, every movable, was an artistic masterpiece; a fortune, as fortunes used to be counted even in this land of affluence, had been lavished in the mere furnishing of a house which the palaces of nobles and princes of other times had contributed to embellish.

"My husband," Mrs. Strange went on, "bought this house for me, and let me furnish it after my own fancy. After it was all done, we neither of us liked it, and when he died, I felt as if he had left me in a tomb here."

"Eveleth," said her mother, "you ought not to speak so before Mr. Homos. He will not know what to think of you, and he will go back to Altruria with a very wrong idea of American women."

At this protest, Mrs. Strange seemed to recover herself a little. "Yes," she said, "you must excuse me. I have no right to speak so. But one is often much franker with foreigners than with one's own kind, and, besides, there is something—I don't know what!—that will not let me keep the truth from you."

She gazed at me entreatingly, and then, as if some strong emotion swept her from her own hold, she broke out:

"He thought he would make some sort of atonement to me, as if I owed none to him! His money was all he had to do it with, and he spent that upon me in every way he could think of, though he knew that money could not buy anything that was really good, and that, if it bought anything beautiful, it uglified it with the sense of cost, to every one who could value it in dollars and cents. He was a good man, far better than people ever imagined, and very simple-hearted and honest, like a child, in his contrition for his wealth, which he did not dare to get rid of; and though I know that, if he were to come back, it would be just as it was, his memory is as dear to me as if—"

She stopped, and pressed in her lip with her teeth, to stay its tremor. I was painfully affected. I knew that she had never meant to be so open with me, and was shocked and frightened at herself. I was sorry for her, and yet I was glad, for it seemed to me that she had given me a glimpse, not only of the truth in her own heart, but of the truth in the hearts of a whole order of prosperous people in these lamentable conditions, whom I shall hereafter be able to judge more leniently, more justly.

I began to speak of Altruria, as if that were what our talk had been leading up to, and she showed herself more intelligently interested concerning us, than any one I have yet seen in this country. We appeared, I found, neither incredible nor preposterous to her; our life, in her eyes, had that beauty of right living which the Americans so feebly imagine, or imagine not at all. She asked what route I had come by to America, and she seemed disappointed and aggrieved that we placed the restrictions we have felt necessary upon visitors from the plutocratic world. Were we afraid, she asked, that they would corrupt our citizens, or mar our content with our institutions? She seemed scarcely satisfied when I explained, as I have explained so often here, that the measures we had taken were taken rather in the interest of the plutocratic world, than of the Altrurians; and alleged the fact that no visitor from the outside had ever been willing to go home again, as sufficient proof that we had nothing to fear from the spread of plutocratic ideals among us. I assured her, and this she easily imagined, that the better known these became, the worse they appeared to us; and that the only concern our Priors felt, in regard to them, was that our youth could not conceive of them in all their enormity, but, in meeting plutocratic people, and seeing how estimable they often were, they would attribute to their conditions the inherent good of human nature. I said that our own life was so logical, so directly reasoned from its economic and political premises, that they could hardly believe the plutocratic life was often an absolute *non sequitur* of the plutocratic premises. I confessed that this error was at the bottom of my own wish to visit America, and study those premises for myself.

"And what has your conclusion been?" she said, leaning eagerly toward me, across the table between us, laden with the maps and charts we had been examining for the verification of the position of Altruria, and my own course here, by way of England.

I heard a slight sigh escape Mrs. Gray, which I interpreted as an expression of the fatigue she might well feel, for it was already past twelve o'clock; and I made it the pretext for an instant escape.

"You have seen the meaning and purport of Altruria so clearly," I said, "that I think I can safely leave you to guess the answer to that question."

She laughed, and did not try to detain me, now, when I offered my hand for good-night. I fancied her mother took leave of me coldly, and with a certain effect of inculpation.

A. HOMOS.

[*To be concluded in the September issue.*]

LETTERS OF AN ALTRURIAN TRAVELLER.

BY W. D. HOWELLS.

A PLUTOCRATIC TRIUMPH.

XI.

New York, April 20, 1894.

My dear Cyril:

It is long since I wrote you, and you have had reason enough to be impatient of my silence. I submit to the reproaches of your letter, with a due sense of my blame; whether I am altogether to blame, you shall say after you have read this.

I cannot yet decide whether I have lost a great happiness, the greatest that could come to any man, or escaped the worst misfortune that could befall me. But such as it is, I will try to set the fact honestly down.

I do not know whether you had any conjecture, from my repeated mention of a lady whose character greatly interested me, that I was in the way of feeling any other interest in her than my letters expressed. I am no longer young, though at thirty-five an Altrurian is by no means so old as an American at the same age. The romantic ideals of the American women which I had formed from the American novels had been dissipated; if I had any sentiment toward them, as a type, it was one of distrust, which my very sense of the charm in their inconsequence, their beauty, their brilliancy, served rather to intensify. I thought myself doubly defended by that difference between their civilization and ours, which forbade any reasonable hope of happiness in a sentiment for them, tenderer than that of the student of new and strange effects in human nature. But we have not yet, my dear Cyril, reasoned the passions, even in Altruria.

After I last wrote you, a series of accidents, or what appeared so, threw me more and more constantly into the society of Mrs. Strange. We began to laugh at the fatality with which we met everywhere, at teas, at lunches, at dinners, at evening receptions, and even at balls, where I have been a great deal, because, with all my thirty-five years, I have not yet outlived that fondness for dancing which has so often amused you in me. Wherever my acquaintance widened among cultivated people, they had no inspiration but to ask us to meet each other, as if there were really no other woman in New York who could be expected to understand me. "You must come to lunch (or tea, or dinner, whichever it might be), and we will have her. She will be so much interested to meet you."

But perhaps we should have needed none of these accidents to bring us together. I, at least, can look back, and see that, when none of them happened, I sought occasions for seeing her, and made excuses of our common interest in this matter and in that, to go to her. As for her, I can only say that I seldom failed to find her at home, whether I called upon her nominal day or not, and more than once the man who let me in said he had been charged by Mrs. Strange to say that, if I called, she was to be back very soon; or, else, he made free to suggest that, though Mrs. Strange was not at home, Mrs. Gray was; and then I found it easy to stay until Mrs. Strange returned. The good old lady had an insatiable curiosity about Altruria, and, though I do not think she ever quite believed in our reality, she at least always treated me kindly, as if I were the victim of an illusion that was thoroughly benign.

I think she had some notion that your letters, which I used often to take with me, and read to Mrs. Strange and herself, were inventions of mine; and the fact that they bore only an English postmark, confirmed her in this notion, though I explained that in our present passive attitude toward the world outside, we had yet no postal relations with other countries, and, as all our communication at home was by electricity, that we had no letter post of our own. The very fact that she belonged to a purer and better age in America disqualified her to conceive of Altruria; her daughter, who had lived into a full recognition of the terrible anarchy in which the conditions have ultimated here, could far more vitally imagine us, and to her, I believe, we were at once a living reality. Her perception, her sympathy, her intelligence, became more and more to me, and I escaped to them oftener and oftener, from a world where any Altrurian must be so painfully at odds. In all companies here, I am aware that I have been regarded either as a good joke, or a bad joke, according to the humor of the listener, and it was grateful to be taken seriously.

From the first, I was sensible of a charm in her, different from that I felt in other American women, and impossible in our Altrurian women. She had a deep and almost tragical seriousness, masked with a most winning gaiety, a light irony, a fine scorn that was rather for herself than for others. She had thought herself out of all sympathy with her environment; she knew its falsehood, its vacuity, its hopelessness; but she necessarily remained in it, and of it. She was as much at odds in it as I was, without my poor privilege of criticism and protest, for, as she said, she could not set herself up as censor of things that she must keep on doing as other people did. She could have renounced the world, as there are ways and means of doing, here; but she had no vocation to the religious life, and she could not feign it, without a sense of sacrilege. In fact, this generous, and magnanimous, and gifted woman was without that faith, that trust in God, which comes to us from living His law, and which I wonder any American can keep. She denied nothing; but she had lost the strength to affirm anything. She no longer tried to do good from her heart, though she kept on doing charity in what she said was a mere mechanical impulse from the belief of other days, but always with the ironical doubt that she was doing harm. Women are nothing by halves, as men can be, and she was in a despair which no man can realize, for we have always some if or and, which a woman of the like mood casts from her in wild rejection. Where she could not clearly see her way to a true life, it was the same to her as an impenetrable darkness.

You will have inferred something of all this, from what I have written of her before, and from words of hers that I have reported to you. Do you think it so wonderful, then, that in the joy I felt at the hope, the solace which my story of our life seemed to give her, she should become more and more precious to me? It was not wonderful, either, I think, that she should identify me with that hope, that solace, and should suffer herself to lean upon me, in a reliance infinitely sweet and endearing. But what a fantastic dream it now appears!

I can hardly tell you just how we came to own our love to each other; but one day I found myself alone with her mother, with the sense that Eveleth had suddenly withdrawn from the room, at the knowledge of my approach Mrs. Gray was strongly moved by something; but she governed herself, and, after giving me a tremulous hand, bade me sit.

"Will you excuse me, Mr. Homos," she began, "if I ask you whether you intend to make America your home, after this?"

"Oh, no!" I answered, and I tried to keep out of my voice the despair with which the notion filled me. I have sometimes had nightmares, here, in which I thought that I was an American by choice, and I can give you no conception of the rapture of awakening to the fact that I could still go back to Altruria, that I had not cast my lot with this wretched people. "How could I do that?" I faltered; and I was glad to perceive that I had imparted to her no hint of the misery which I had felt at such a notion.

"I mean, by getting naturalized, and becoming a citizen, and taking up your residence amongst us."

"No," I answered, as quietly as I could, "I had not thought of that."

"And you still intend to go back to Altruria?"

"I hope so; I ought to have gone back long ago, and if I had not met the friends I have in this house—" I stopped, for I did not know how I should end what I had begun to say.

"I am glad you think we are your friends," said the lady, "for we have tried to show ourselves your friends. I feel as if this had given me the right to say something to you, that you may think very odd."

"Say anything to me, dear lady," I returned. "I shall not think it unkind, no matter how odd it is."

"Oh, it's nothing. It's merely that— that when you are not here with us, I lose my grasp on Altruria ; and—and I begin to doubt—"

I smiled. "I know! People here have often hinted something of that kind to me. Tell me, Mrs. Gray, do Americans generally take me for an impostor?"

"Oh, no!" she answered, fervently. "Everybody that I have heard speak of you has the highest regard for you, and believes you perfectly sincere. But—"

"But what?" I entreated.

"They think you may be mistaken."

"Then they think I am out of my wits —that I am in an hallucination!"

"No, not that," she returned. "But it is so very difficult for us to conceive of a whole nation living, as you say you do, on the same terms as one family, and no one trying to get ahead of another, or richer, and having neither inferiors nor superiors, but just one dead level of equality, where there is no distinction, except by natural gifts, and good deeds, or beautiful works. It seems impossible, it seems ridiculous"

"Yes," I confessed, "I know that it seems so to the Americans."

"And I must tell you something else, Mr. Homos, and I hope you won't take it amiss. The first night when you talked about Altruria, here, and showed us how you had come, by way of England, and the place where Altruria ought to be on our maps, I looked them over, after you were gone, and I could make nothing of it. As far as I could see, Australia and New Zealand occupied the place that Altruria ought to have had on the map."

"Australia and New Zealand are more like Altruria than any other countries of the plutocratic world, in their constitution," I said, "and perhaps that was what made them seem to occupy our place."

"No, it wasn't that; it couldn't have been, for I didn't know that they were like Altruria. I can't explain it—I never could. I have often looked at the map since, but it was no use."

"Why," I said, "if you will let me have your atlas—"

She shook her head. "It would be the same again, as soon as you went away." I could not conceal my distress, and she went on : "Now, you mustn't mind what I say. I'm nothing but a silly old woman, and Eveleth would never forgive me if she could know what I've been saying."

"Then Mrs. Strange isn't troubled, as you are, concerning me?" I asked, and I confess my anxiety attenuated my voice almost to a whisper.

Mrs. Gray shook her head vaguely. "She won't admit that she is. It might be better for her if she would. But Eveleth is very true to her friends, and that—that makes me all the more anxious that she should not deceive herself."

"Oh, Mrs. Gray!" I could not keep a certain tone of reproach out of my words.

She began to weep. "There! I knew I should hurt your feelings. But you mustn't mind what I say. I beg your pardon! I take it all back—"

"Ah, I don't want you to take it back! But what proof shall I give you that there is such a land as Altruria! If the darkness implies the day, America must imply Altruria. In what way do I seem false, or mad, except that I claim to be the citizen of a country where people love one another as the first Christians did?"

"That is just it," she returned. "Nobody can imagine the first Christians, and do you think we can imagine anything like them in our own day?"

"But Mrs. Strange—she imagines us, you say?"

"She thinks she does; but I am afraid she only thinks so, and I know her better than you do, Mr. Homos. I know how enthusiastic she always was, and how unhappy she has been since she has lost her hold on faith, and how eagerly she has caught at the hope you have given her of a higher life on earth than we live here. If she should ever find out that she was wrong, I don't know what would become of her. You mustn't mind me ; you mustn't let me wound you by what I say!"

"You don't wound me, and I only thank you for what you say ; but I entreat you to believe in me. Mrs. Strange has not deceived herself, and I have not deceived her. Shall I protest to you, by all that is sacred, that I am really what I told you I was ; that I am not less, and that Altruria is infinitely more, happier, better, gladder, than any words of mine can say? Shall I not have the happiness to see your daughter to-day? I had something to say to her, something—and now I have so much more! If she is in the house, will not you send to her? I can make her understand—"

I stopped at a certain expression which I fancied I saw in Mrs. Gray's face.

"Mr. Homos," she began, so very seriously that my heart trembled with a vague misgiving, "sometimes I think you had better not see my daughter any more."

"Not see her any more?" I gasped.

"Yes; I don't see what good can come of it, and it's all very strange, and uncanny. I don't know how to explain it; but, indeed, it isn't anything personal. It's because you are of a state of things so utterly opposed to human nature, that I don't see how—I am afraid that—"

"But I am not uncanny to *her*?" I entreated. "I am not unnatural, not incredible—"

"Oh, no; that is the worst of it. But I have said too much; I have said a great deal more than I ought. But you must excuse it: I am an old woman. I am not very well, and I suppose it's that makes me talk so much."

She rose from her chair, and I perforce rose from mine, and made a movement toward her.

"No, no," she said, "I don't need any help. You must come again soon, and see us, and show that you've forgotten what I've said." She gave me her hand, and I could not help bending over it, and kissing it. She gave a little, pathetic whimper. "Oh, I *know* I've said the most dreadful things to you."

"You haven't said anything that takes your friendship from me, Mrs. Gray, and that is what I care for." My own eyes filled with tears, I do not know why, and I groped my way from the room. Without seeing any one in the obscurity of the hallway, where I found myself, I was aware of some one there, by that sort of fine perception that makes us know the presence of a spirit.

"You are going?" a whisper said. "Why are you going?" And Eveleth had me by the hand, and was drawing me gently into the dim drawing-room that opened from the place. "I don't know all my mother has been saying to you. I had to let her say something; she thought she ought. I knew you would know how to excuse it."

"Oh, my dearest!" I said, and why I said this I do not know, or how we found ourselves in each other's arms.

"What are we doing?" she murmured.

"You don't believe I am an impostor, an illusion, a visionary!" I besought her, straining her closer to my heart.

"I believe in you, with all my soul!" she answered.

We sat down, side by side, and talked long. I did not go away the whole day. With a high disdain of convention, she made me stay. Her mother sent word that she would not be able to come to dinner, and we were alone together at table, in an image of what our united lives should be. We spent the evening in that happy interchange of trivial confidences that lovers use in symbol of the unutterable raptures that fill them. We were there in what seemed an infinite present, without a past, without a future.

Society had to be taken into our confidence, and Mrs. Makely saw to it that there were no reserves with society. Our engagement was not quite like that of two young persons, but people found in our character and circumstance an interest far transcending that felt in the engagement of the most romantic lovers. Some note of the fact came to us by accident, as one evening when we stood near a couple, and heard them talking. "It must be very weird," the man said; "something like being engaged to a materialization." "Yes," said the girl, "quite the Demon Lover business, I should think." She glanced round, as people do, in talking, and, at sight of us, she involuntarily put her hand over her mouth. I looked at Eveleth; there was nothing expressed in her face but a generous anxiety for me. But so far as the open attitude of society toward us was concerned, nothing could have been more flattering. We could hardly have been more asked to meet each other than before; but now there were entertainments in special recognition of our betrothal, which Eveleth said could not be altogether refused, though she found the ordeal as irksome as I did. In America, however, you get used to many things. I do not know why it should have been done, but in the society columns of several of the great newspapers, our likenesses were printed, from photographs procured I cannot guess how, with descriptions of our persons as to those points of coloring, and carriage, and stature, which the pictures could not give, and with biographies such as could be ascertained in her case and imagined in mine. In some of the society papers, paragraphs of a surpassing scurrility appeared, attacking me as an impostor, and aspersing the motives of Eveleth in her former marriage, and treating her as a foolish crank, or an audacious flirt. The goodness of her life, her self-sacrifice and works of benevolence counted for no more against these wanton attacks than the absolute inoffensiveness of my own; the writers knew no harm of her, and they knew nothing at all of me; but they devoted us to the execration of their readers simply because we formed apt and ready themes for paragraphs. You may judge of how wild they were in their aim when some of them denounced me as an Altrurian plutocrat!

We could not escape this storm of notoriety; we had simply to let it spend its fury. When it began, several reporters of both sexes came to interview me, and questioned me, not only as to all the facts of my past life, and all my purposes in the future, but as to my opinions of hypnotism, eternal punishment, the Ibsen drama, and the tariff reform. I did my best to answer them seriously, and certainly I answered them civilly; but it seemed from what they printed that the answers I gave did not concern them, for they gave others for me. They appeared to me for the most part kindly and well-meaning young people, though vastly ignorant of vital things. They had apparently visited me with minds made up, or else their reports were revised by some controlling hand, and a quality injected more in the taste of the special journals they represented, than in keeping with the facts. When I realized this, I refused to see any more reporters, or to answer them, and then they printed the questions they had prepared to ask me, in such form that my silence was made of the same damaging effect as a full confession of guilt upon the charges.

The experience was so strange and new to me that it affected me in a degree I was unwilling to let Eveleth imagine. But she divined my distress, and when she divined that it was chiefly for her, she set herself to console and reassure me. She told me that this was something every one here expected, in coming willingly or unwillingly before the public; and that I must not think of it at all, for certainly no one else would think twice of it. This, I found was really so, for when I ventured tentatively to refer to some of these publications, I found that people, if they had read them, had altogether forgotten them; and that they were, with all the glare of print, of far less effect with our acquaintance, than something said under the breath in a corner. I found that some of our friends had not known the effigies for ours which they had seen in the papers; others made a joke of the whole affair, as the Americans do with so many affairs, and said that they supposed the pictures were those of people who had been cured by some patent medicine, they looked so strong and handsome. This, I think, was a piece of Mr. Makely's humor in the beginning; but it had a general vogue, long after the interviews and the illustrations were forgotten.

I linger a little upon these trivial matters because I shrink from what must follow. They were scarcely blots upon our happiness; rather they were motes in the sunshine which had no other cloud. It is true that I was always somewhat puzzled by a certain manner in Mrs. Gray, which certainly was from no unfriendliness for me: she could not have been more affectionate to me, after our engagement, if I had been really her own son; and it was not until after our common kindness had confirmed itself upon the new footing that I felt this perplexing qualification on it. I felt it first one day when I found her alone, and I talked long and freely to her of Eveleth, and opened to her my whole heart of joy in our love. At one point she casually asked me how soon we should expect to return from Altruria after our visit; and at first I did not understand.

"Of course," she explained, "you will want to see all your old friends, and so will Eveleth, for they will be her friends, too; but if you want me to go with you, as you say, you must let me know when I shall see New York again."

"Why," I said, "you will always be with us!"

"Well, then," she pursued with a smile, "when shall *you* come back?"

"Oh, never!" I answered. "No one ever leaves Altruria, if he can help it, unless he is sent on a mission."

She looked a little mystified, and I went on: "Of course, I was not officially authorized to visit the world outside, but I was permitted to do so, to satisfy a curiosity the Priors thought useful; but I have now had quite enough of it, and I shall never leave home again."

"You won't come to live in America?"

"God forbid!" said I, and I am afraid I could not hide the horror that ran through me at the thought. "And when you once see our happy country, you could no more be persuaded to return to America than a disembodied spirit could be persuaded to return to the earth."

She was silent, and I asked: "But, surely, you understood this, Mrs. Gray?"

"No," she said, reluctantly. "Does Eveleth?"

"Why, certainly!" I said. "We have talked it over a hundred times. Hasn't she—"

"I don't know," she returned, with a vague trouble in her voice and eyes. "Perhaps I haven't understood her exactly. Perhaps—but I shall be ready to do whatever you and she think best. I am an old woman, you know; and you know, I was born here, and I should feel the change."

Her words conveyed to me a delicate reproach; I felt for the first time that, in my love of my own country, I had not considered her love of hers. It is said that the Icelanders are homesick when they leave their world of lava and snow; and I ought to have remembered that an American might have some such tenderness for his atrocious conditions, if he were exiled from them forever. I suppose it was the large and wide mind of Eveleth, with its openness to a knowledge and appreciation of better things, that had suffered me to forget this. She seemed always so eager to see Altruria, she imagined it so fully, so lovingly, that I had ceased to think of her as an alien; she seemed one of us, by birth as well as by affinity.

Yet, now, the words of her mother, and the light they threw upon the situation, gave me pause. I began to ask myself questions which I was impatient to ask Eveleth, so that there should be no longer any shadow of misgiving in my breast; and yet I found myself dreading to ask them, lest by some perverse juggle I had mistaken our perfect sympathy in all things for a perfect understanding.

Like all cowards who wait a happy moment for the duty that should not be suffered to wait at all, I was destined to have the affair challenge me, instead of seizing the advantage of it that instant frankness would have given me. Shall I confess that I let several days go by, and still had not spoken to Eveleth, when, at the end of a long evening—the last long evening we passed together—she said:

"What would you like to have me do with this house while we are gone?"

"Do with this house?" I echoed; and I felt as if I were standing on the edge of an abyss.

"Yes; shall we let it, or sell it; or what? Or give it away?" I drew a little breath at this; perhaps we had not misunderstood each other, after all. She went on: "Of course, I have a peculiar feeling about it, so that I wouldn't like to get it ready, and let it furnished, in the ordinary way. I would rather lend it to some one, if I could be sure of any one who would appreciate it; but I can't. Not one! And it's very much the same when one comes to think about selling it. Yes, I should like to give it away for some good purpose, if there is any in this wretched state of things! What do you say, Aristide?"

She always used the French form of my name, because she said it sounded ridiculous in English, for a white man, though I told her that the English was nearer the Greek in sound.

"By all means, give it away," I said. Give it to some public purpose. That will at least be better than any private purpose, and put it somehow in the control of the State, beyond the reach of individuals or corporations. Why not make it the foundation of a free school for the study of the Altrurian polity and economy?"

She laughed at this, as if she thought I must be joking. "It would be droll, wouldn't it, to have Tammany appointees teaching Altrurianism?" Then she said, after a moment of reflection: "Why not? It needn't be in the hands of Tammany. It could be in the hands of the United States; I will ask my lawyer if it couldn't; and I will endow it with money enough to support the school handsomely. Aristide, you have hit it!"

I began: "You can give *all* your money to it, my dear—" But I stopped at the bewildered look she turned on me.

"All?" she repeated. "But what should we have to live on, then?"

"We shall need no money to live on, in Altruria," I answered.

"Oh, in Altruria! But when we come back to New York?"

It was an agonizing moment, and I felt that shutting of the heart which blinds the eyes and makes the brain reel. "Eveleth," I gasped, "did you expect to return to New York?"

"Why, certainly!" she cried. "Not at once, of course. But after you had seen all your friends, and made a good, long visit— Why surely, Aristide, you don't understand that I— You didn't mean to *live* in Altruria?"

"Ah!" I answered. "Where else could I live? Did you think for an instant that I could live in such a land as this?" I saw that she was hurt, and I hastened to say, "I know that it is the best part of the world outside of Altruria; but, oh, my dear, you cannot imagine how horrible the notion of living here seems to me. Forgive me! I am going from bad to worse. I don't mean to wound you. After all, it is your country, and you must love it. But, indeed, I could not think of living here. I could not take the burden of its wilful, hopeless misery on my soul. I must live in Altruria, and you, when you have once seen my country, *our* country, will never consent to live in any other!"

"Yes," she said, "I know it must be very beautiful; but I hadn't supposed— and yet I ought—"

"No, dearest, no! It was I who was to blame, for not being clearer from the first. But that is the way with us! We can't imagine any people willing to live anywhere else when once they have seen Altruria; and I have told you so much of it, and we have talked of it together so often, that I must have forgotten you had not actually known it. But listen, Eveleth! We will agree to this. After we have been a year in Altruria, if you wish to return to America, I will come back and live with you here."

"No, indeed!" she answered, generously. "If you are to be my husband," and here she began with the solemn words of the Bible, so beautiful in their quaint English, "'whither thou goest, I will go, and I will not return from following after thee. Thy country shall be my country, and thy God my God.'"

I caught her to my heart, in a rapture of tenderness, and the evening that had begun for us so forbiddingly, ended in a happiness such as not even our love had known before. I insisted upon the conditions I had made, as to our future home, and she agreed to them gaily, at last, as a sort of reparation which I might make my conscience, if I liked, for tearing her from a country which she had willingly lived out of for the far greater part of the last five years.

But when we met again, I could see that she had been thinking seriously.

"I won't give the house absolutely away," she said. "I will keep the deed of it myself, but I will establish that sort of school of Altrurian doctrine in it, and I will endow it, and when we come back here, for our experimental sojourn, after we've been in Altruria a year, will take up our quarters in it,—I won't give the whole house to the school,—and we will lecture on the later phases of Altrurian life to the pupils. How will that do?"

She put her arms round my neck, and I said that it would do admirably; but I had a certain sinking of the heart, for I saw how hard it was even for Eveleth to part with her property.

"I'll endow it," she went on, "and I'll leave the rest of my money at interest here; unless you think that some Altrurian securities—"

"No; there are no such things!" I cried.

"That was what I thought," she returned; "and as it will cost us nothing while we are in Altruria, the interest will be something very handsome by the time we get back, even in United States bonds."

"Something handsome!" I cried. "But, Eveleth, haven't I heard you say yourself that the growth of interest from dead money was like—"

"Oh, yes; that!" she returned. "But you know you have to take it. You can't let the money lie idle; that would be ridiculous; and then, with the good purpose we have in view, it is our *duty* to take the interest. How should we keep up the school, and pay the teachers, and everything?"

I saw that she had forgotten the great sum of the principal, or that, through life-long training and association, it was so sacred to her that she did not even dream of touching it. I was silent, and she thought that I was persuaded.

"You are perfectly right in theory, dear, and I feel just as you do about such things; I'm sure I've suffered enough from them; but if we didn't take interest for your money, what should we have to live on?"

"Not *my* money, Eveleth!" I entreated.

"Don't say *my* money!"

"But whatever is mine is yours," she returned, with a wounded air.

"Not your money; but I hope you will soon have none. We should need no money to live on in Altruria. Our share of the daily toil of all will amply suffice for our daily bread and shelter."

"In Altruria, yes. But how about America? And you have promised to come back here in a year, you know. Ladies and gentlemen can't share in the daily toil, here, even if they could *get* the toil, and where there are so many out of work, it isn't probable they could."

She dropped upon my knee, as she spoke, laughing, and put her hand under my chin, to lift my fallen face.

"Now, you mustn't be a goose, Aristide, even if you *are* an angel! Now, listen! You *know*, don't you, that I hate money just as badly as you?"

"You have made me think so, Eveleth," I answered.

"I hate it and loathe it. I think it's the source of all the sin and misery in the world; but you can't get rid of it at a blow. For if you gave it away, you might do more harm than good with it."

"You could destroy it," I said.

"Not unless you were a crank," she returned. "And that brings me just to the point. I know that I'm doing a very queer thing to get married, when we know so little, really, about you," and she accented this confession with a laugh that was also a kiss. "But I want to show people that we are just as practical as anybody; and if they can know that I have left my money all in United States bonds, they'll respect us, no matter what I do with the interest. Don't you see? We can come back, and preach and teach Altrurianism, and as long as we pay our way, nobody will have the right to say a word. Why, Tolstoy himself doesn't destroy his money, though he wants other people to do it. His wife keeps it, and supports the family. You *have* to do it."

"He doesn't do it willingly."

"No. And *we* won't. And after a while —after we've got back, and compared Altruria and America from practical experience, if we decide to go to live there altogether, I will let you do what you please with the hateful money. I suppose we couldn't take it there with us."

"No more than you could take it to heaven with you," I answered solemnly; but she would not let me be altogether serious about it.

"Well, in either case, we could get on without it, though we certainly could not get on without it, here. Why, Aristide, it is essential to the influence we shall try to exert for Altrurianism; for if we came back here, and preached the true life without any money to back us, no one would pay any attention to us. But if we have a good house waiting for us, and are able to entertain nicely, we can attract the best people, and—and—really do some good."

I rose in a distress which I could not hide. "Oh, Eveleth, Eveleth!" I cried. "You are like all the rest, poor child. You are the creature of your environment, as we all are. You cannot escape what you have been. It may be that I was wrong to wish or expect you to cast your lot with me in Altruria, at once and forever. It may be that it is my duty to return here with you after a time, not only to let you see that Altruria is best, but to end my days in this unhappy land, preaching and teaching Altrurianism; but we must not come as prophets to the comfortable people, and entertain nicely. If we are to renew the evangel, it must be in the life and the spirit of the First Altrurian: we must come poor to the poor; we must not try to win any one, save through his heart and his conscience; we must be simple and humble as the least of those that Christ bade follow Him. Eveleth, perhaps you have made a mistake! I love you too much to wish you to suffer even for your good. Yes, I am so weak as that! I did not think that this would be the sacrifice for you that it seems, and I will not ask it of you. I am sorry that we have not understood each other, as I supposed we had. I could never become an American; perhaps you could never become an Altrurian. Think of it, dearest! Think well of it, before you take the step which you cannot recede from. I hold you to no promise; I love you so dearly that I cannot let you hold yourself. But you must choose between me and your money—no; not me! —but between love and your money. You cannot keep both."

She had stood listening to me; now she cast herself on my heart, and stopped my words with an impassioned kiss. "Then there is no choice for me. My choice is made, once for all." She set her hands against my breast, and pushed me from her. "Go, now! But come again to-morrow. I want to think it all over again. Not that I have any doubt; but because you wish it—you wish it, don't you?—and because I will not let you ever think I acted upon an impulse, and that I regretted it."

"That is right, Eveleth! That is like *you*," I said, and I took her into my arms for good-night.

The next day, I came for her decision, or rather for her confirmation of it. The man who opened the door to me, met me with a look of concern and embarrassment. He said Mrs. Strange was not at all well, and had said he was to give me the letter he handed me. I asked, in taking it, if I could see Mrs. Gray, and he answered that Mrs. Gray had not been down yet, either, but he would go and see. I was impatient to read my letter, and I made I know not what vague reply, and I found myself, I know not how, on the pavement, with the letter open in my hand. It began abruptly without date or address:

"You will believe that I have not slept, when you read this.

"I have thought it all over again, as you wished, and it is all over between us.

"I am what you said, the creature of my environment. I cannot detach myself from it; I cannot escape from what I have been.

"I am writing this with a strange coldness, like the chill of death in my very soul. I do not ask you to forgive me; I have your forgiveness already. Do not forget me; that is what I ask. Remember me as the unhappy woman who was not equal to her chance when heaven was opened to her: who could not choose the best, when the best came to her.

"There is no use writing; if I kept on forever, it would always be the same cry of shame, of love.

"EVELETH STRANGE."

I reeled as I read the lines. The street seemed to weave itself into a circle around me. But I knew that I was not dreaming, that this was no delirium of my sleep.

It was three days ago, and I have not tried to see her again. I have written her a line, to say that I shall not forget her, and to take the blame upon myself. After all, I expected the impossible of her.

I have yet two days before me until the steamer sails; we were to have sailed together, and now I shall sail alone.

I will try to leave it all behind me forever; but while I linger out these last long hours here, I must think, and I must doubt.

Was she, then, the poseuse that they said? Had she really no heart in our love? Was it only a pretty drama she was playing, and were those generous motives, those lofty principles which seemed to actuate her, the poetical qualities of the play, the graces of her pose? I cannot believe it. I believe that she was truly what she seemed, for she had been that even before she met me. I believe that she was pure and lofty in soul as she appeared; but that her life was warped to such a form by the false conditions of this sad world, that, when she came to look at herself again, after she had been confronted with the sacrifice before her, she feared that she could not make it without in a manner ceasing to be.

She—

But I shall soon see you again; and, until then, farewell.

A. HOMOS.

[THE END.]

LIBRARY OF
LAMAR STATE COLLEGE OF TECHNOLOGY